DOING IRISH LOCAL HISTORY

DOING IRISH LOCAL HISTORY
PURSUIT AND PRACTICE

edited by Raymond Gillespie and Myrtle Hill

The Institute of Irish Studies
The Queen's University of Belfast

First published 1998
Reprinted 1999
The Institute of Irish Studies
The Queen's University of Belfast

This book has received support from the Cultural Diversity Programme of the
Community Relations Programme of the Community Relations Council which
aims to encourage acceptance and understanding of cultural diversity.
The views expressed do not necessarily reflect those of the
NI Community Relations Council.

British Library Cataloguing-In-Publication Data.
A catalogue record for this book is available from the British Library.

ISBN 0 85389 676 3

Set in Ehrhardt
Printed by W. & G. Baird Ltd, Antrim

Front cover: Detail from Etching in Layers series by Anne M. Anderson

CONTENTS

List of illustrations   vi

Preface   vii

Notes on Contributors   viii

Introduction   1–4

I The pursuit of Irish local history

Raymond Gillespie   An historian and the locality   7–23

P. J. Duffy   Locality and changing landscape:
                       geography and local history   24–46

Linda May Ballard   The folklorist and local history   47–61

Myrtle Hill   Reading the past: literature and local history   62–78

II The practice of Irish local history

Leslie Clarkson   Doing local history: Armagh in the
                       eighteenth century   81–96

W. H. Crawford   The study of townlands in Ulster   97–115

Nick Brannon   The built heritage and the local historian   116–127

John Lynch   The comparative aspect in local studies   128–147

LIST OF ILLUSTRATIONS

Shifting landscapes: townlands in the barony of Coole   11

Processes in the making of the landscape   27

Field names in Loughloon, county Mayo   33

Civil and Catholic parishes in the diocese of Clogher   35

Population decline by electoral division, county Monaghan   41

The locations of 'views' in Irish prints published up to 1850   43

View of Armagh in 1810   82

Part of the Down Survey of county Meath   102

Aerial photograph of Rathtrillick Rath, county Armagh   119

Reconstructed 1674 Coleraine town house at the
Ulster Folk and Transport Museum   122

The illustrations are reproduced by permission of the following: pp. 26, 33, 35, 41 and 43, the Geography Department, the National University of Ireland, Maynooth; p. 82, the Armagh County Museum; p. 119 and p. 122, crown copyright. The poem 'Epic' is reproduced courtesy of the trustees of the estate of Patrick Kavanagh and the extract from *Told in Gath* by Max Wright by kind permission of the author.

PREFACE

Books, like people, have their individual and sometimes complex histories. This one is no exception to that generalisation. The essays here began life as papers given to a conference held at the Queen's University campus at Armagh in October 1995 as part of the celebrations of the 150th anniversary of the founding of Queen's University, Belfast, and the bicentenary of the establishment of St Patrick's College, Maynooth, now National University of Ireland, Maynooth. Both institutions have been in the forefront of shaping local historical study in their respective parts of Ireland. Such a conference was an appropriate way of celebrating a common anniversary and bringing people from all parts of Ireland together around their passion for the study of the local past.

We owe a great debt to all those who made the conference the success it was, especially to Peter Collins and Gary Sloan who shouldered most of the practical arrangements on that occasion. A grant from the Cultural Traditions Group of the Northern Ireland Community Relations Council made the conference possible, and they have generously continued their support with a subvention towards the publication of this collection of essays. That publication was managed by the Institute of Irish Studies at Queen's with its customary expedition. Between these two events the contributors have been both good humoured and patient. Their efforts will be appreciated by all those who do local history in Ireland.

R.G.
M.H.

NOTES ON CONTRIBUTORS

Linda May Ballard is Curator of Textiles at the Ulster Folk and Transport Museum. She has achieved international recognition as an authority on the folklore of Northern Ireland and has published widely on various aspects of the history of custom, belief and oral history of the region, and of its textiles and material culture.

Nick Brannon is Assistant Director, Recording the Built Heritage in the Environment and Heritage Service of Northern Ireland. He has published numerous archaeological reports and is an authority on the archaeology of the Ulster Plantation.

Leslie Clarkson is Professor of Social History at The Queen's University of Belfast. He is the author of a number of works on eighteenth-century demography and on Armagh, including (with Margaret Crawford) *Ways to Wealth*, on the Cust family in the town.

W. H. Crawford was development officer with the Federation for Ulster Local Studies and is an authority on the social and economic development of eighteenth-century Ulster.

P. J. Duffy is Associate Professor of Geography at the National University of Ireland, Maynooth. He is best known for his work on the development of the south Ulster landscape, including *Landscapes of south Ulster: a parish atlas of the diocese of Clogher* (1993).

Raymond Gillespie teaches local history at the National University of Ireland, Maynooth and is the author of a number of books on early modern Ireland as well as being the editor of studies of Mayo, Longford, Cavan and the Ulster borderlands.

Myrtle Hill formerly taught local history at the Institute of Continuing Education, The Queen's University of Belfast and is now Director of the Centre for Women's Studies there. She has written widely on religion in nineteenth-century Ireland.

John Lynch is a teaching fellow in the Department of Economic and Social History at The Queen's University of Belfast, where he specialises in local studies and emigration studies. His research interests include urban and labour history.

INTRODUCTION

By any measure local studies of all kinds are booming in Ireland. A great diversity of themes is now under scrutiny from a regional or more local perspective. Within local studies the most vibrant activity is probably the practice of local history. An explosion of local history societies, local journals and magazines all testify to the health of local history in the parishes and counties of Ireland. The Federation for Ulster Local Studies in Ulster and the Federation of Local History Societies in the rest of the island are both evidence of the desire of local societies to come together and share common concerns about the problem of doing local history in an Irish context. In the past the main difficulty for the beginner in local history was 'how to find out' about a particular local topic or place. As studies have multiplied and guides to sources have become available, finding information about a locality has become rather less of a hurdle than it used to be, although we have a great deal to learn, especially about the effective use of non-documentary sources such as folklore, architecture and visual material.

The greater ease with which appropriate sources can now be identified, together with their relative accessibility in archives and libraries, has inevitably given rise to other challenges for the local historian in Ireland. It is now possible to accumulate a large volume of information about individual areas within Ireland. Even for small units, such as the townland, the amount which can be discovered by an intensive trawl through the surviving evidence is staggering. We now need to turn our minds to the problem of how this material can be meaningfully interpreted and attractively presented to those who read local history. We need to remember those actively working as local historians who want to compare the experience of differing parts of the country as well as those who are simply interested in a particular locality. To reproduce the raw data may be interesting to a few, but to most it appears boring at best and at worst it seems entirely irrelevant.

This volume of essays offers some suggestions as to how local history in Ireland might be 'done' so as to make it more appealing and interesting to both the reader and the practitioner. It is not a manual. It does not supply a model to be followed nor does it pretend to answer all the questions. Rather it is an attempt to ask some pertinent questions about Irish local history and the best way to approach it. This is done by considering two dimensions of local historical study. The first we have termed 'the pursuit of Irish local history'. This section reviews the subject matter of Irish local history and suggests avenues of enquiry that might profitably be pursued in an attempt to answer some of those questions. In particular, the essays in the first section try to explore the sort of questions we can now ask of our sources, questions which do not necessarily lead to a replication of the studies of parishes, counties, schools and businesses that have often been done in the past. Four essays, each written from the perspective of a different discipline or approach to local history, try to look at the subject from different angles. From the perspective of an historian, Raymond Gillespie's essay points out that the usual preoccupation of local history of the study of particular places does not allow us to understand the local experience in the past as fully as we should be able to. It is only when we realise that the sense of place was created by the people who lived in that place that we can begin to fully appreciate the nature of the local past. Local history is not then about a place but about the people who lived in that place over past time. This insight enables us to link together the many regions of Ireland and the national experience through the eyes of those people living in a place who moved between differing worlds or 'communities of interest'. Such an understanding helps us to ask a new series of questions about our evidence for the local past, concentrating not just on the place but on the attitudes and values of the people who lived in it. The following essays explore the local past from two rather different perspectives. P. J. Duffy explores the understanding of places as created by people by considering the humanised landscape of the locality from a geographer's point of view. The result is a geographical framework for local studies which is considerably more complex than that which local historians have normally used in their studies. The physical landscape with its building types, road networks and farms, combined with the mental landscape created by placenames and customs, become one method of understanding how people in the past lived out their daily lives in local places. Moreover, since these landscapes are not static they provide another means of measuring the responses of groups of people and individuals to the changes in the world around them.

Another way of thinking about how we do local history is to consider previously neglected kinds of sources and thereby develop new approaches to the subject. Linda May Ballard argues for the importance of folklore on a variety of levels as a method of approaching the past. Oral traditions not only provide information about aspects of life which in other circumstances can be difficult to find material on, it is also the case that in using the folk tales people remembered and retold as a source, we begin to understand a great deal more about the cultural climate of the past. Stories about fairies and ghosts are ways of understanding the reality of the supernatural world which was much more real to those in the past than to many people today. A similar point of departure, that of fictional works, enables Myrtle Hill to show the importance of literature in understanding the histories of localities. Sometimes these are established works of the literary canon, such as those by Anthony Trollope and William Carleton, but more ephemeral works are important also in conveying a sense of the past. However, none of these approaches to the past stands alone. The sources discussed by Ballard and Hill may appear different to those which Duffy and Gillespie deal with but, in fact, they are complementary to each other, the difference being one of perspective rather than of substance. The message contained in folklore, for instance, can only be understood when it has been compared with the documentary sources. Thus by considering the real diversity in the range of sources available, we can begin to understand something of the complexity of the study of local history. There is scope and need for a variety of approaches to the available evidence, just as there is scope and need to combine a wide range of sources so that we can reveal not just the physical worlds of localities in past time, but also come to understand the mental worlds of the people who inhabited those localities through time. As local historians we need to prepare ourselves to ask new questions of all the available sources, both those well-known, well-used documents and those lesser-used materials whose importance is only now being realised.

The second part of this book approaches the same problem of how we do local history in Ireland in a slightly different way. This we have entitled 'the practice of Irish local history', for it is more concerned with the practicalities of writing local history. Two essays, those by W. H. Crawford and Leslie Clarkson, offer some practical advice about how to do local history, ranging from setting the task to locating the sources and finally to presenting the findings. Leslie Clarkson explores a town, eighteenth-century Armagh, by taking a series of approaches to the evidence which he has used in writing about that town in the past. First, there is the possibility of simply counting the differing types of inhabitants of the town; second, there is the possibility of trying to set those people in a social context, that of the community. It is also possible to approach that community, not in aggregate, but through the eyes of one family, and the example used here is the Custs. An exploration of the world of Annaritta Cust leads us into a more complex world of her relations and their associated families. All these are possible ways of doing local history. W. H. Crawford, on the other hand, provides a way into the rural world through the history of one of its most fundamental units, the townland. Using the valuation of Ireland made by Richard Griffith in the middle of the nineteenth century as a base line, we can explore a series of themes of fundamental importance to the evolution of rural society. The study of the organisation of estates and the creation of farms, changes in farming practices, housing, communications and marketing are all important methods of examining local societies in the past. While Crawford's essay uses Ulster examples, the same themes are central to the exploration of the local past in every part of the island of Ireland, and similar sources exist for use in that exploration.

In the final two essays of this section, Nick Brannon and John Lynch address two rather more specialised problems in the practice of local history, one concerned with sources and the other with methods. Local historians are well acquainted with archaeological field monuments, but the built heritage in the wider sense is often overlooked. Yet the built heritage provides one of the key pieces of evidence for reconstructing the past, as P. J. Duffy's essay in the first part of this volume suggests. Lack of information about how to find sources to research this heritage has proved an obstacle in the past, but Nick Brannon here provides a guide to the work of the Environment and Heritage Service which maintains a record of such matters. Finally, John Lynch demonstrates why local historians in the practice of local history must not be myopic in their studies. If local history is to be both interesting and meaningful, those who practice it must set their own studies in context. Those who write local history must ask the question *why* regions have their own characteristics, and then should describe these particular characteristics by comparison with those of other regions. These four essays provide new insights on the practice of local history by advocating new ways of approaching problem issues, suggesting various alternatives in writing up the results of research, and prompting consideration of sources which perhaps we have not thought about, or could not find, before.

This volume is not about prescribing a new programme for local studies. It is rather a response by a number of people from various backgrounds, interested in and working in the area of local history, to what they perceive as the challenges presented in the study of local history today. It is not the intention to provide ready answers to the problem of how to do local history in Ireland but rather to provoke all practitioners of that subject into asking some more searching questions about what they are doing and how they might do it better.

I

The pursuit of Irish local history

AN HISTORIAN AND THE LOCALITY

Raymond Gillespie

To judge from the growing number of Irish local history societies and the recent explosion in the volume of local historical publications, there are more people in Ireland today 'doing local history' than ever before. It might be worth stopping to ask what are we doing? Even a brief survey of the results of this activity would produce a bewildering variety of answers. Not surprisingly, histories of families abound but there are a myriad of other topics also being tackled: local studies of place-names, folklore and topography are all in a healthy state. If it is difficult to generalise about what is being done, might it be more helpful to ask how it is being done? The answers again seem obvious. More people than ever before are visiting local libraries to consult older local studies and are making their way to the record offices to search for primary sources relevant to their own area. Part of the reason why this task is so popular is that it now much easier to locate primary sources than it was ten years ago. Several helpful guides to assist in the quest have been published, many prompted by the growth of interest in genealogy, and most of the courses available in local history spend a good deal of time tackling the problem of locating sources.[1]

There is no doubt that sources are of the first importance in the study of local history. The strength of many of the great nineteenth-century local studies, such as Carrigan's history of the diocese of Ossory, Burke's history of Clonmel or Reeves on the diocese of Down and Connor, was their encyclopaedic knowledge of the source material for their own area.[2] It is perhaps a measure of the greatness of these works, and the continuing demand for them, that they managed to combine a mastery of the evidence with the ability to make the subject matter interesting to those outside the area being studied. This is an aspiration which few of us lesser mortals can hope to achieve. For many of us the temptation when constructing the history of a locality is to rely overly much on the sources without much in the way of interpretation or explanation. Lists of nineteenth-century local residents from Griffith's valuation or names from attendance registers of the local national school at the beginning of the twentieth century, printed as part of a modern local study, more often than not fail to catch the imagination of any but the most parochial reader. Sources do not speak for themselves. They have to be enticed to give up their secrets. As the great French rural historian Marc Bloch once expressed it, sources are like witnesses at a trial; the cross-examination by the historian must contain the right questions to make them yield up what they know.[3] Asking questions then must be a large part of the 'how' of local history. It is the key to the proper use of the 'historical imagination' which should bring the past to life and make local studies of relevance beyond the boundaries of the townland, parish, town or county which is their primary focus.

I

To pose questions on what local historians should do and how they might do it raises a myriad of issues which local historians in Ireland have not yet begun to consider. For most practitioners of local history their subject almost seems to define itself – the study of a small place, or locality, in the past. In their eyes it is the scale of the study which differentiates their work from that of 'national' historians. In this way of thinking the fundamental questions which local historians must ask of their sources are about place. Of course the immediate cry which this approach prompts is 'which place?' Here there is no agreement. County, diocese and parish are all, of course, newcomers to the world of local history for before their discovery local history was being written in medieval Ireland in a different way in the form of genealogies, annals and local chronicles. In the native Irish tradition it was the lordship which provided the inspiration for questions about place. This tradition survived into the early eighteenth century in texts such as the 'Genealogical history of the O'Reillys' and Roderic O'Flaherty's description of hIar Connacht and has been more recently rediscovered by some local societies such as Cumann Seanchas Breifne and Teathbha. The county, an area much beloved by many Irish local historians, has only been used by them for a relatively brief period of time. The county in most of Ireland is a creation of the sixteenth and seventeenth centuries and hence only began to be used by historians as a unit of study towards the end of the seventeenth century. As the new settlers tried to explore the world in which they had settled, they produced county descriptions with substantial historical components. First, in the 1680s, William Molyneux collected county descriptions for the abortive atlas planned by London publisher Moses Pitt.[4] An even more ambitious scheme was embarked on in the 1740s for the Physico-Historical Society under whose auspices histories and descriptions of counties Down, Cork, Waterford and Kerry were produced by Walter Harris and Charles Smith.[5] By the end of the eighteenth century the Royal Dublin Society was at work producing its Statistical Surveys. All these works drew on English traditions of local history-writing stretching back to the sixteenth century. The philosophy which inspired them was tied to the expansion of central authority into the regions (hence the interest in powerful local families) and a growing interest in local antiquities. It was this tradition also which heavily influenced the writing of Irish local history in the nineteenth century. E. P. Shirley's 1879 history of Monaghan was written by a man educated at Eton and Oxford and with estates both at Lough Fea and in Warwickshire. It is hardly surprising that it was dedicated to 'the nobles and gentlemen of Monaghan'.[6] As local history societies sprang up in the late nineteenth century it was usually under the patronage of a powerful local landlord. One of the oldest of these societies, which many others imitated, was the Kildare Archaeological Society founded in 1891 under the patronage of the duke of Leinster and his brother the redoubtable Lord Walter Fitzgerald.

The influential position of the county as a unit of study in Irish local history in the past should not blind us to alternative ways of writing local history. In the nineteenth century a better-educated Catholic clergy (due mainly to the establishment of St Patrick's College, Maynooth in 1795) turned its hands to writing local history. Instead of a county focus they looked to the diocese and parish as units of study. As the Catholic church grew in confidence in the course of the nineteenth century it needed a history which established its credentials in the modern world of rival denominational orthodoxies. Thus many of the diocesan histories of the nineteenth century, such as that for Down and Connor by Monsignor O'Laverty and that for Ossory by Canon Carrigan, are parish-by-parish tours showing how the succession of Catholic parish priests descended from Saint Patrick and how, in effect, theirs was the true church of Ireland.[7] As the introduction to Cogan's 1862 history of the diocese of Meath explained, it was written 'for love of religion and country'. In more recent days the effects of Vatican II are discernible in the writing of this type of local history. The three volumes on the diocese of Killaloe by the late Monsignor Ignatius Murphy, published in the 1990s, are more concerned with the core of religious life such as worship, prayer and pastoral work than with the organisation of the church or the succession of parish priests.

II

There is therefore a plethora of different questions which the local historian can ask about 'place' with a consequent confusion in the sort of answers which are obtained. The simple idea of studying places as a way of doing local history is fraught with problems. The result is often a series of unconnected studies, which have little hope of being connected because of the different concepts behind them, and which do little to illuminate the workings of the past. Moreover, if there are few connections to link different local studies together there are even fewer to connect those studies with what is some-times called 'national history'. It seems we are doomed to live in a compart-mentalised world of 'particular places' with no hope of seeing the wood for innumerable trees, saplings and shrubs, each with its own characteristics.

In an attempt to avoid this sort of problem let us think again about the idea of place which seems to be such a defining characteristic of local history in Ireland. Almost as soon as we begin to think about places we fall victim to the creations of both the ecclesiastical and governmental bureaucracies of the nineteenth century. We think of a mesh of townlands, parishes, baronies and counties all delineated with precision on the Ordnance Survey maps of the mid nineteenth century. We are happy to use these boundaries both for the convenience of available maps and the fact that they were also the basis of information-gathering by central government. Thus the population and agricultural statistics fit neatly into a spatial framework. Yet to accept this landscape frozen in time is to lose sight of one of the main tasks of the histo-rian: to explain change over time. That neatly drawn administrative land-scape was, in some places, of fairly recent creation.

Let us take one example to illustrate the point. The townlands which com-prise the site of what is now the town of Newport in county Mayo were described in the Books of Survey and Distribution of the 1660s as Ballyveghane, Carrowbane and Knockmagee although there was not yet a town on the site. In a rental of the town and its surroundings in 1744 a new townland of eighty-nine acres appears called Bleachyard. By 1774 two more townlands have appeared in the area, Barrickhill and Weaversquarter. The old names are also there. The changes are fairly simply explained in terms of the history of the estate. In 1700 the property, held by the duke of Ormond, was leased to a Thomas Medlycott who in turn sub-let it to a Mr Pratt who began to build a new town on the site (hence Newport Pratt, the older name of the modern town). By the 1720s part of this strategy of developing the town was to invite Quaker weavers into the region and this led to the begin-nings of the linen trade and the creation of bleachyards. The newly created

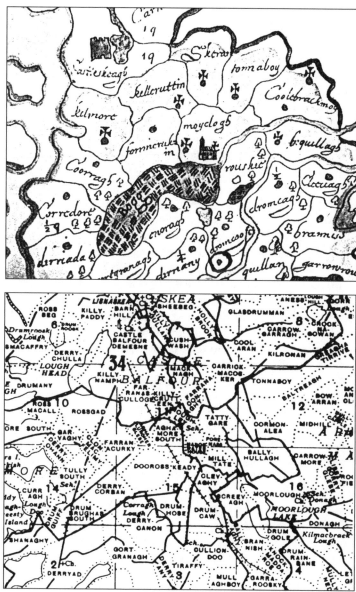

Shifting landscapes: townlands in the barony of Coole, Co. Fermanagh in 1609 (above, Public Record Office, London, M.P.F. 38) and today. While there is substantial continuity, new townlands have been created by cutting away bog and subdividing old units.

townland name records that the Quakers left in the 1730s but the linen trade
thrived and weavers arrived, settling in 'Weavers' Quarter'. Finally, also as
part of the development strategy for the town, an army barracks was constructed on Barrickhill.[8]

The lesson which we should learn from this Mayo example is that the
administrative landscape recorded by the Ordnance Survey in the nineteenth
century was not immutable. Townlands were created, and others disap-
peared, over time in response to social, economic and possibly even political
changes in the local world. However this was not imposed by some set of
impersonal forces. It was done by local inhabitants. The boundaries of such
units and their names were remembered as long as they were useful and dis-
carded when they were not. Today the same is true of micro-toponymics.
Field names, for instance, have a relatively short life before they become dis-
carded in favour of new names more relevant to changes brought about by
changing agricultural practices or the arrival of new owners. Before the rise
of estate mapping in the eighteenth century we can see a little of this process
at work. Those who wished to know the boundaries of a townland or a parish
had to ask the oldest inhabitants. The normal way of doing this was to sum-
mon an inquisition and ask the oldest inhabitants of an area about the local
topography. Perhaps the most ambitious attempt in this direction was the
1654 Civil Survey which described, parish by parish, how boundaries ran
along rivers, from stone to bush and across bogs.[9] However the process also
operated on a much smaller scale as juries were summoned to resolve disputes on individual estates where it was alleged that one man had trespassed
on another's property.[10] Why people remembered boundaries is a difficult
question to answer. Sometimes particular events fixed boundaries in peoples'
minds. The annual riding of the franchises in Dublin, for example, was
undertaken to ensure that the boundaries of the city's authority was kept
fresh in at least some minds. Tenants also had good cause to remember the
bounds of their property to ensure they were not encroached upon. Before
the advent of the Ordnance Survey, places and their boundaries were defined
and identified not on paper but in peoples' minds. As P. J. Duffy's essay
reminds us, the landscape was strongly humanised.

III

What lies behind the questions about place which have so preoccupied local
historians is another set of questions even more fundamental: the questions
about the people who created those places and lived in them. Of the three
organising principles of people, place and time which historians of all kinds

use in presenting the past, it is people that should be the main focus of the Irish local historian's efforts. We might therefore see local history as the study of people in a particular place over time. This is at least implicit in H. P. R. Finberg's 1952 formulation of the task of the local historian: 'the business of the local historian then, as I see it, is to re-enact in his own mind and to portray for his readers the origin, growth, decline and fall of a local community'.[11] If people are to be central to the task of local history then rather than study individuals we are more likely to want to study groups, or communities of individuals. The definition of 'community' has bedevilled local history. This is not a purely academic quibble. Perhaps we might surmount the problem by saying that the people whom local historians wish to study are those living together with something in common.

Two elements of this definition, people and common interests, call for comment here. Irish local histories have never lacked people in their pages but they have always been people of a rather exalted kind. Parish histories have often been dominated by lists of Catholic parish priests or Church of Ireland rectors. Outside the parish history there has often been a tendency to demonstrate the high IQ of a particular region or its political acumen by recording the names of famed sons and daughters who originated in the county, townland or town. Finally there is the record of the famous who have passed through. There are many Irish local histories whose description of the Repeal Movement or the Land War is a newspaper report of a speech given by Daniel O'Connell or Charles Stewart Parnell in their own region. Such approaches tell us little about the experience of all the people in a particular place. Studies which put people at their core must attempt to study all the people from landlord to landless labourer and from priest or minister to atheist. This is an enormous task, hence the importance of utilising common interests as an interpretative tool. We need to find some way of categorising these people into manageable units to study them more clearly. Here we might try to break them up according to the things which they had in common or 'communities of interest'. [12]

Let me try to define five 'communities of interest' or things which both drew some people together and also set them apart from others: the estate, social groupings, family, religion and politics. The list could, of course, be extended almost infinitely depending on the needs of the particular local study. The community of the estate was created by the commonality of living on a particular estate. This might be expressed in many ways. Until the middle of the nineteenth century those living on an estate might meet at regular gatherings such as the manorial courts which were often associated with hospitality provided by the landlord. Obligations to grind corn at the manor mill provided another common meeting place. More paternalistic landlords might also organise entertainment for their tenants at Christmas or Easter. Similarly, when labour services were part of the rent tenants were drawn together at harvest time to work on the demesne lands. The importance of the big house as an employer and as a source of charity in times of need should not be forgotten. Such a community was not always a tranquil one. Disputes frequently emerged between tenants and many of these fell to be resolved by the landlord. The result was that each estate quickly acquired its own character, determined by the temperament of the landlord and the balance of power between landlord and tenants.[13] The community of the estate was not an undifferentiated one. There was within it a hierarchy of leaseholders, tenants at will, and those who held no land at all. Such a hierarchy was demonstrated in many ways ranging from church seating to manner of dress. Clearly, large farmers who had common interests showed some solidarity with each other. In some parts of the country this was demonstrated in the sharing of labour and resources at times of the agricultural year when a pooling of resources was required. Again some were more exposed to market forces than others and that reality bound the more commercialised together. The family provides a good example of a community of interest that transcended a single geographical region. Webs of kinship linked people from often diverse geographical and social backgrounds. Patterns of migration mean that a 'local' study of one family might extend over a geographically large area and after the nineteenth century might well reach to North America or Canada. Yet these would not have been remote links. The significance of the remittance money from emigrants to the local economy was often considerable.

Two other communities of interest are perhaps more difficult to define precisely. A shared sense of religious belief derived from meeting together on a Sunday morning at various forms of worship was a communal bond. There may have been a geographical framework to those meetings such as the parish in the Church of Ireland or Catholic traditions, but in the case of Methodists or Presbyterians that spatial commonality was much less well pronounced. Such communal bonds might express themselves in all sorts of cultural ways. Different senses of history and even of geography might be characteristic of religious groupings. Thus in the midlands members of one religious denomination might call a settlement Edgeworthstown while another would refer to it by its older name of Mostrim. However, we should avoid being prescriptive here for in 1641 it was the Church of Ireland minister who remembered the Gaelic name for Virginia in county Cavan when the Catholics had forgotten it. Finally, politics shaped communities of interest in localities. This is an aspect usually ignored by local historians who continue to take their understanding of politics from national studies. Yet great national movements such as the Land League or Catholic Emancipation were underpinned by local organisations whose membership and activities were reported in local newspapers.[14] Politics also provided an occasion for people to meet together. Indeed local O'Connellite politics were as much underpinned by dinners and toasts as they were by serious discussions of Emancipation or Repeal. This opens up another world of sociability at a local level which was quasi-political in its organisation. Orange lodges, Masonic meetings and Tenants Defence leagues were all places where people of similar outlooks might meet and exchange ideas. Reading societies, or even the communal reading of newspapers so well documented from nineteenth-century Ireland, must have fulfilled similar functions.

It is important to realise that such 'communities of interest' were not static affairs. Individuals moved about a great deal in the past and it is now clear that their horizons were not limited by the townland, parish or even region. Even a cursory glance at a nineteenth-century local newspaper would reveal news not just about the locality but about Ireland, Britain and indeed Europe and America. Thus such 'communities of interest' not only overlapped considerably, they also had links to a wider world, and provided a link between national and local affairs. In the case of the church, each parish in the nineteenth century was not an isolated unit. Catholic priests were trained in Maynooth, the Church of Ireland ministers in Dublin and the clergy of the various dissenting churches in Belfast. These ministers brought to the localities the benefit of their central training and aspects of the shared culture of their fellow trainees. The religious literature, such as the catechism, which affected the lives of those who worshipped in their churches, was centrally disseminated through these local clergy. Again landlords performed a similar role as 'brokers' between the local and national worlds, bringing ideas from Dublin or elsewhere to bear on local problems. The village of Monivea in county Galway, for instance, was transformed in the eighteenth century by the activities of its landlord, Robert French, who implemented ideas he had become familiar with while in Dublin as a member of the Irish parliament.[15]

All of this is not to argue that every region in Ireland was identical and passively received ideas from the metropolis. There was clearly enormous variation within the country as a whole. The fact that ideas travelled from Dublin to the localities, and vice versa, does not account for such variation. A crucial factor was the way such ideas were received within local societies. There were profound differences in the way in which brokers might function in a region of large compact estates as compared with a society made up of

small scattered ones, between areas of highly differentiated religious allegiances and regions where the denominational balance was more clearly
defined. Areas which had different patterns of emigration, either seasonal or
more permanent, and other experiences were similarly diverse in their
response to external influences. Here Estyn Evans' concept of 'personality'
may be helpful in interpreting diversity.[16] Historical experiences and the
activities of the various communities of interest in a locality could determine
a great deal of its 'personality'. The area where, in the nineteenth century,
industrialised, Protestant Ulster met the more agrarian Leinster is a case in
point. Here was a region with its own personality which transcended county
boundaries, being composed of parts of Down, Monaghan, Armagh and
Louth. It differed from all the regions around it. It was one of the last pre-
serves of toryism and the Irish language, and in the eighteenth century had a
vibrant tradition of poets.[17] Clearly its reception of the ideas imported by the
'brokers', whether clergy or landlords, would be rather different from that of
surrounding areas.

IV

Local history therefore is primarily about people in places over time. It is not
simply a set of questions about one place in the past. People create their own
places, differing from each other by the configuration of their 'communities
of interest'. Elements from a centralised government and church all combined with local needs and requirements to create a distinct 'personality' for
a region. With this idea of local history in mind we should ask again how
might we 'do local history' in Ireland. Clearly, when we begin any local study
the first thing to do is to find the stage on which the actors will appear, that
is to find a region to study. This should be something the actors when they
appear will recognise, so it must be a 'human' unit. Before the advent of the
county newspaper, the GAA, and county-based electoral units in the nineteenth century, few outside the elite probably identified with their county.
There were other worlds, two of which are explored by Leslie Clarkson and
W. H. Crawford in their essays in this volume. River valleys, for example, are
probably more important than we might think since they are usually topo-
graphically significant and have relatively dense settlement. Similarly, as suggested above, the south Ulster/north Leinster region is one with which its
inhabitants have felt an affinity that has been sustained over time.

   Many local historical studies assume that the reader is familiar with the
place to be written about. This is not always so. A map of the local area is
always required. Moreover since the past often has a foreign topography it is

important to outline the contours of that world. We need to know how that landscape looked in the past; was it good land or bad, were there buildings on it and if so what sort were they and how were they arranged? Here it is important to remember that the landscape is not an unchanging world and landscape change reflects changes in the wider social world. Changes in the landscape, which from the work of W. G. Hoskins and others we now appreciate to be an important piece of evidence, are significant.[18] Moreover these changes in the landscape were made by the people who occupied that world. We need to know a great deal more about how landscapes were understood by the people who inhabited them in the past. Maps and travellers' descriptions clearly go some way to providing accounts of how contemporaries understood their world but folklore and place-name studies can be even more revealing. Behind prominent topographic features or archaeological features there are often stories. Sometimes these are religious in content: a holy well originating with the patron saint of the parish striking a rock in a Moses-like gesture to bring forth water or cupmarks from a saint kneeling to pray. One French traveller in the 1640s passing through the Cork area was told that a ruined round tower had been built by St Finbar without lime 'then it was lopped or half destroyed by the same saint who jumped from top to bottom of it and imprinted the mark of his foot on a flint stone'. It was at this place that women now gathered to pray because it was a holy place.[19] In such stories we can see not only order being placed on the landscape. We can also see the invisible world of saints and demons being related to the tangible, and religious belief being made concrete in particular times and places. Similarly stories of the fianna or Fionn Mac Cumhaill are often used to explain topographic features such as the Giant's Causeway or the origins of both Lough Neagh and the Isle of Man.

Questions about place, as I have already suggested, are only preliminaries to the real questions which local historians should be grappling with, questions about people. It is therefore necessary to populate this past landscape. Perhaps the most basic question to begin with here is how many people lived in this region and how did that change over time? For the nineteenth century the census returns, used with some care, will answer this question but the further back in time we go the more difficult the problem becomes. Bare statistics are not very interesting and we need to relate them to every-day life. Behind the census figures lie families, and local knowledge combined with reconstruction from the 1901 census and parish registers help us to see something of the dramatically different responses of people in a place to events, such as the Famine, which are usually described in the abstract.[20] It is clear that there were enormous differences in response to events such as the Famine even over small areas. It is only by studying families in a locality that we will understand whether this was the result of mortality or migration patterns. Moreover we do not need a catastrophic event such as the Famine to point out significant variants in the history of small areas. Assembling lists of surnames, for example, would enable us to chart the local history of migration and determine whether townlands or other areas represent 'open' or 'closed' societies. Townlands such as Cloonfush in county Galway were in the early nineteenth century a closed world with little land changing hands and the only way outsiders entered into that world was by marriage. However most marriages took place between families within the townland. In Roscommon, by contrast, some townlands retained a core of families from the eighteenth century but new families also appeared. In other places, such as Ballyrashane in north Antrim, a much more dramatic change in population has taken place since the eighteenth century.[21] Explaining why such divergent changes have taken place is an important task for local historians.

After migration, marriage and death seem to be the main demographic variables. Parish register data provides readily accessible data for both. Simple counts of deaths will often reveal patterns of local epidemic and food shortages but here we can go a good deal further in the understanding of the history of death. We need to know a good deal more about how people thought about death and for this the local graveyard is a much underused resource. Changing patterns of funeral monuments, together with their inscriptions, can tell us a good deal about attitudes to death and how people wished to be remembered.[22] Unlike death, marriage is a matter of choice and as such provides an important insight into the way in which local societies worked and how people interacted within a region. Whom an individual married is not only an important indicator of social organisation, but also reveals how individuals viewed their world. Some English studies have suggested that before the revolution in transport in this century people tended to marry within well-defined 'cultural regions' and we need to look more carefully at these in an Irish context by mapping marriage patterns.[23]

Simple aggregate numbers of people in a landscape are not a very good indicator of the social world. People have to be related to the resources in an area. County Tipperary can clearly support more people in a rather different style of life than north county Mayo and this reality influences how population should be analysed. It also raises other questions of how resources are shared within a community. This brings us back to the landlord and his role in sharing out resources through leasing policies on estates. Sometimes special treatment was given to some people specially brought into areas to improve them. In the late eighteenth century Ulster weavers were imported into the west of Ireland and given preferential status in newly created towns such as Westport, Newport, Monivea and Mountshannon. Others were given favourable leases in the countryside. Others were more marginalised in that world but they too have histories. Women and the poor, for example, rarely appear in local studies but they too have important histories.[24]

The allocation of resources often led to tensions within local communities and how these stresses were resolved should be an important part of the local historian's study. The police files for the nineteenth century, especially the period of the Land War, provide the material not only for the crimes being investigated and the motives which lay behind them, but also the social fabric within which they were embedded. Here we need to use a wide range of sources to provide different perspectives on the problem. Official records, newspaper reports and folklore all provide differing perspectives on patterns of crime and criminality.[25] Not all social tensions make their way into such exalted documents. Some events, while criminal in the eyes of the law, were clearly tolerated or ignored by local communities in the past and these require more investigation.[26] Much of the evidence here lies in the difficult world of folklore, the possibilities of which are discussed in Linda May Ballard's essay in this volume.

Local historians over the last thirty years or so have spent some time discussing these social and economic problems and to a lesser extent have directed some of their efforts to political life. What remains as a major lacuna in local history is an understanding not of this material world but of the mental worlds of those who lived in the past. This has received little attention in parish histories which have concentrated on the institutional history of religion. There are innumerable histories of parishes and of individual churches that deal with the succession of clergy and church buildings. These are important but many fall victim to the difficulty of 'particular places': they try to explain what is unique to an area rather than what was normal in that kind of society. One example of this in the Catholic tradition might be the 'penny catechism' which is usually ignored because it was regarded as part of national history. Yet more than any other manifestation of the church this had an impact on the lives of those who lived in individual parishes throughout the country. We need to know a great deal more about what went on in individual churches on a Sunday morning and about why people chose to go there and participate in rituals such as communion.[27] One way in which we might approach the problem of what the institutional church offered to individuals in the localities is to focus not on institutions but on what we might describe as 'religious sociability'. People gathered at many religious functions apart from Sunday services. Within the institutional context there were sodalities, men's meetings and bible study groups which also met a religious need. Gatherings at holy wells for prayer or participation in pilgrimages are also important here. What is important is not simply to catalogue holy well sites and places of pilgrimage but to try to understand more clearly why people went there and what they did while there. Here we need to look more carefully at unusual sources such as depictions in art and popular novels, some of which are discussed below by Myrtle Hill, as well as more traditional autobiographies and institutional archives to appreciate more fully how the sacred and the secular intertwined in the past.

A concentration on the official church and the things which it organised can, however, be distorting. Beyond the world of pulpit and pew there was another supernatural world represented in beliefs about ghosts, fairies, charms and folk cures. The same people who listened to the exposition of orthodox doctrine on Sundays also believed in things for which the official church had little time. How did they square the world of the church with the other supernatural world represented in folklore? We need not see the two as diametrically opposed even if some in the institutional churches in the nineteenth century clearly did so. Rather than accepting the theology of Maynooth, Trinity College Dublin or Assemblies Theological College in Belfast, people in local places took notice of what their clergy had to say to them but also modified those orthodoxies to reflect their own experiences, traditions and local circumstances. Folklore may provide some of the answers to the local historian's questions on such topics but as yet we have barely begun to ask the questions.[28]

If religious belief brought local communities together around a shared view that there was a supernatural world which was active in their every-day world, it is equally important to recognise that religious ideas also divided communities. Why and how this was so has been little studied. We know very little about what each side of the confessional divide thought of the other and how those opinions were formed. We also need to know how deep those divisions ran. It seems clear that various confessional groups in Ireland were not, except in time of severe political or economic crisis, totally polarised. There are therefore limits to confessional division. Local historians can investigate how Protestants and Catholics might co-operate in the past and when and why they were unable to do so.

V

This essay has not tried to set out a complete way of thinking about the local or regional past. The wide agenda which has been sketched out here is not relevant to every study. New questions have to be tailored to meet the specific evidence which emerges every time a new study is begun. What I have tried to do is to sketch out some general principles which might help when trying to frame what a local study might do. In particular I have tried to stress the importance of having people rather than places as the central focus of local studies. To do this means asking a vast range of new questions about how local and regional societies in the past worked. To answer these questions we will need to go back to the same sources used by the nineteenth-century local historians, combine them with a consideration of things they would have regarded as irrelevant such as folklore, visual evidence and popular literature and look at the full range of evidence in ways rather different to those of our predecessors. Only when we do this will our local historical imagination be able to have the free reign it deserves.

1. For example, William Nolan, *Tracing the past* (Dublin, 1982); D. F. Begley, *Irish geneaology: a record finder* (Dublin, 1981); John Grenham, *Tracing your Irish ancestors* (Dublin, 1992).

2. William Carrigan, *The history and antiquities of the diocese of Ossory* (4 vols, Dublin, 1905); W. P. Burke, *History of Clonmel* (Waterford, 1907); William Reeves, *The ecclesiastical antiquities of Down, Connor and Dromore* (Dublin, 1847). All these have been reprinted within the last ten years.

3. Marc Bloch, *The historian's craft* (Manchester, 1992), pp. 52-4. The metaphor is particularly apt for Emmanuel Le Roy Ladurie, *Montaillou: Cathars and Catholics in a French village 1294-1324* (London, 1978) which was itself written from court records.

4. Now in Trinity College, Dublin, MS 883.

5. Walter Harris, *The antient and present state of the county of Down* (Dublin, 1744); Charles Smith, *The ancient and present state of the county and city of Cork* (2 vols, Dublin, 1750); Charles Smith, *The antient and present state of the county and city of Waterford* (Dublin, 1746); Charles Smith, *The antient and present state of the county of Kerry* (Dublin, 1756).

6. E. P. Shirley, *The history of the county of Monaghan* (London, 1879).

7. James O'Laverty, *An historical account of the diocese of Down and Connor ancient and modern* (4 vols, Dublin, 1878-84).

8. I have taken this example from the second chapter of J. P. McDermott, 'An examination of the accounts of James Moore, land agent, Newport Pratt, Co Mayo, 1742-65' MA (Local History) thesis, St Patrick's College, Maynooth, 1994. A large database exists at the Northern Ireland Place-Names Project at the Celtic Studies Department, the Queen's University of Belfast which may yield further examples of this.

9. R. C. Simington (ed.), *The civil survey, 1654-6* (10 vols, Dublin, 1931-61).

10. For example Edmund Curtis (ed.), *Calendar of Ormond deeds* (6 vols, Dublin, 1932-43), vi, pp. 126, 132, 134, 140, 141, 145.

11. Developed in H. P. R. Finberg, *The local historian and his theme* (Leicester, 1952) from which the quotation is taken. For a critique of this approach, J. D. Marshall, *The tyranny of the discrete* (London, 1997) chs. 4-6.

12. Some of these ideas are further developed in the introduction of Raymond Gillespie and Gerard Moran (eds), *'A various country': essays in Mayo history, 1500-1900* (Westport, 1987).

13. W. H. Crawford, 'The significance of the landed estate in Ulster' in *Irish economic and social history* xvii (1990).

14. For an excellent example of the recreation of a local political activity see Fergus O'Ferrall's essay in Raymond Gillespie and Gerard Moran (eds), *Longford: essays in county history* (Dublin, 1991).

15. Denis A. Cronin, *A Galway gentleman in the age of improvement: Robert French of Monivea* (Dublin, 1995).

16. E. E. Evans, *The personality of Ireland* (rev. ed. Dublin, 1991).

17. For this case in more detail, Raymond Gillespie and Harold O'Sullivan (eds), *The borderlands: essays on the history of the Ulster-Leinster border* (Belfast, 1989); Raymond Gillespie (ed.), *Cavan: essays on the history of an Irish county* (Dublin, 1995).

18. Most recently reissued and updated as W. G. Hoskins, *The making of the English landscape* ed. Christopher Taylor (London, 1992).

19. T. Crofton Croker (ed.), *The tour of M. de la Boullaye le Gouez in Ireland, 1644* (London, 1832), p. 30.

20. For two examples of studies which follow families over time, Robert Scally, *The end of hidden Ireland: rebellion, famine and emigration* (Oxford, 1995); P. H. Gulliver and Marilyn Silverman, *Merchants and shopkeepers: an historical anthropology of an Irish market town* (Toronto, 1995).

21. William Gacquin, *Roscommon before the famine: the parishes of Kiltoom and Cam* (Dublin, 1996). The Cloonfush study by Gabriel O'Connor is in Denis Cronin, Paul Connell, Brian Ó Dálaigh (eds), *Irish townland studies in local history* (Dublin, 1998) pp. 69–92. For another good case study of migration W. A. Macafee, 'The colonisation of the Maghera region of south Derry during the seventeenth and eighteenth centuries' in *Ulster Folklife* xxiii (1977), pp. 70-91. An important model for these sort of studies is contained in Ruth Finnegan, Michael Drake (eds), *From family tree to family history* (Cambridge 1994), W. T. R. Pryce (ed.), *From family history to community history* (Cambridge, 1994) and John Goldby (ed.), *Communities and families* (Cambridge, 1994).

22. For example Raymond Gillespie, 'Irish funeral monuments and social change, 1500-1700: perceptions of death' in Raymond Gillespie and Brian P. Kennedy (eds), *Ireland: art into history* (Dublin, 1994).

23. See the English evidence in Charles Phythian Adams, *Rethinking English local history* (Leicester, 1987). The idea is further developed in Charles Phythian Adams (ed.), *Societies, cultures and kinship, 1580-1800* (London, 1993).

24. An interesting exception to this generalisation is Maureen Langan-Egan, *Women in Mayo, 1821-50* (Westport, 1996).

25. There are a number of studies which might serve as models here including, W. E. Vaughan, *Sin, sheep and Scotsmen* (Belfast, 1983); Gerard Moran, *The Mayo evictions* (Westport, 1986) and Jarlath Waldron, *Maamtrasna: the murder and the mystery* (Dublin, 1992).

26. For an French example of collective actions in the nineteenth century on this matter, see Alain Corbin, *The village of cannibals* (Oxford, 1992).

27. Two good studies are John Crawford, *St Catherine's parish, Dublin, 1840-1900: portrait of a Church of Ireland community* (Dublin, 1996); and Francis Kelly, *Window on a Catholic parish: Granard, county Longford, 1933-68* (Dublin, 1996).

28. See Linda May Ballard's essay below and Charles Phythian Adams, *Local history and folklore: a new framework* (London, 1975).

LOCALITY AND CHANGING LANDSCAPE: GEOGRAPHY AND LOCAL HISTORY

P. J. Duffy

Geography is a 'territorial' science. It is concerned with the environment, landscapes and place, the meaning and significance of the location and distribution of aspects of the environment. Whatever about the discipline of history in general, local history suggests a clear territorial emphasis in its study. It places a priority on scale and on locality. The local place and its 'localness', where it is and its connection with other places assume considerable importance. In this sense therefore, local history has considerable affinity with geographical studies.

Geography's role in local historical studies may be characterised by its distinctive objectives, methods and sources. Its object of study is the landscape and its morphology; its method is to examine the making of the landscape in the past and the sources it uses help this process by concentrating especially on those with spatial applications. The following discussion will concentrate broadly on these three themes.

I

One could say that the main preoccupation of the geographer is the landscape context of society or community, that is the landscape which *environs* the community. In fact there are also important social and economic aspects in a community's occupation of the landscape which are of interest to the geographer as well; for example, rich and poor have different territorial and landscape expressions. So it could be said that we are also talking of the societal context of the landscape. An additional important aspect of this societal context is the way different groups – whether classes, interest groups, lobbies – read and represent their landscape. There are different layers of meaning in landscape which will be adverted to later.

Landscape and place probably best epitomise the kind of things geographers are interested in. And at the local level, landscape and place assume greater significance for us because local landscapes and places represent the most familiar dimensions to our lives. We are born and bred in local landscapes; we come to know them intimately. The shape, size and texture of our first place probably remains with us always. When we move out of it, we continue to remember it. But we also become familiar with other subsequent places. Local landscapes therefore are the common, every-day places we move around in on a regular basis. They are vastly more significant for us than the broader region or state, parts of which we are only familiar with in an infrequent or incomplete manner. On this basis, therefore, the geographical dimension and the geographer's preoccupation with landscape and place is an important added dimension in local studies and local history. For this reason, geographical studies together with history must form an essential part of the educational foundation for young people in Ireland and the proposal to abandon history and geography as core subjects in the second level Junior Cycle in the Republic is a serious mistake.

Localism, local culture, traditions, songs, customs and stories, all are inherently redolent of the geography of place. Much of this localism is central to the distinctiveness of local landscapes and their sense of place. Local studies often spring from a consciousness of the distinctiveness of a local place, a distinctiveness born of interrelationship of landscape and people over time and a need to understand the meaning and significance of the local place or area through time. One of the founding fathers of geography, Friedrich Ratzel, suggested that while it was possible that he could understand New England without knowing the land, he could never understand it without knowing the Puritan immigrants. Sense of place is both social and territorial: it derives its meaning from society and place, a community in a landscape. The landscape bears the marks or inscriptions of the generations who made, modified and transformed it in the past in its buildings, farms and fields, roads and bridges, churches, trees and hedges. For purposes of understanding, the landscape can be divided into its main ingredients of the physical landscape of environmental quality, the human landscape of settlements, and the community which occupies the place and gives it its identity. Combined in a variety of ways, all these elements help to give each place its varying distinctiveness, called by some geographers the personality of place.

II

A fruitful geographical method of undertaking a local study is to examine the evolution, or making, of its landscape: what were the forces or processes which went into its making? We can classify these into a broad range of social and economic processes in the past which might be considered to have had impacts on the landscape. Thus, to take an agricultural example because agriculture has made such a pervasive contribution to landscape development, market demand for beef and butter for the expanding Atlantic trade in the eighteenth century provoked a regional response in Irish farming. In Munster, especially at local level in the rich pastures of east Cork and the Golden Vale, farmers went into dairying. In landscape terms the repercussions might be seen in investment in rearrangement of fields, in buildings in the countryside, in roads and bridges. At local level, the geographer is concerned to show how the landscape impact of broader market forces was mediated through a range of influences and agencies such as local landowners, middlemen tenants, lesser tenants, merchants and traders, churches and government, all of which in various ways influenced the day-to-day running and shaping of the farm and its landscape.

The shaping of the landscape by past generations clearly is of central concern. The local landscape in which the present generation moves is a legacy of past contributions. Its shape, scale, size and distances are legacies of different economic orders when, for example, mobility was lower and the world was local.

> Events of the past have assembled people in quite different technical and economic conditions and have thus created economies of scale that still determine the optimal marginal movements of factors of production.[1]

The landscape as legacy, therefore, is an important starting concept in local studies. Legacies imply continuities, inertia, as well as slow modifications of earlier contributions. Legacies in the present can be seen as keys to the past. But concentrating exclusively on these inherited qualities of the landscape can be ahistorical in the sense that it can miss out on many processes in the past which have come and gone and left no traces. In some cases relict features in the landscape do reflect aspects of these lost worlds of the past, as for example in the case of the abandoned potato ridges on bleak mountainsides in the west of Ireland, but the flimsy habitations of the poorest classes for hundreds of years have left few clues to their existence.

Figure one attempts to illustrate with examples the major processes which went into the making of the landscape and with suggestions as to how these might be interlinked in their operation. They have been broadly categorised as locational, environmental, economic, cultural, social and ideological processes of change. Each of these processes may be seen to have contributed to landscape development either materially, in the form of, for example, set-

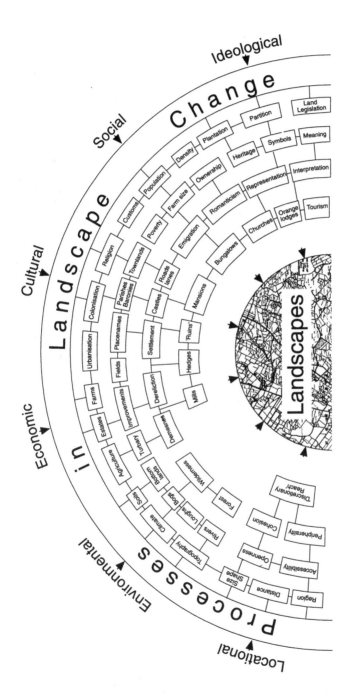

Figure 1: Processes in the making of the landscape. P. J. Duffy

tlement patterns, fields and hedges, townlands, castles, or more indirectly as a consequence of processes such as colonisation, 'improvements', religion, emigration. In this sense, much of the story of local places in the past has a spatial or landscape manifestation. The following pages discuss in turn these various processes of landscape change.

III

'Local-ness' or 'locality' are fundamentally locational qualities. Social and economic processes in the past have been importantly influenced or modified by locational factors. It is impossible to adequately undertake a local study without regard to its locational relationship with other localities and regions, its openness, its resistibility, or its peripherality to change. Locational considerations therefore take account of a broad range of categories to do with an area's strategic position in space and time with regard to impulses for change. Robert Scally, in his study of emigration from a west of Ireland townland, conducted an extended analysis of the significance of Ballykilcline's location in Roscommon and Ireland in the mid nineteenth century: knowledge and isolation were closely connected, leading to the Famine emigrants' understanding and visualisation of the outside world.[2] In geographical studies, the importance of the process of diffusion in understanding the nature of change has long been understood – the diffusion of innovations for example, emanating from a point of origin outwards through a territory. Thus spatial characteristics like distance and location can have an important bearing on the transfer and reception of new ideas. The concept of distance decay reflects the reduced impact of change processes with distance from a centre of diffusion. In an historical sense, empirical evidence would suggest that most impulses for change, either socially or economically, originated in urban centres and filtered outwards into rural hinterlands. So, for example, the Irish language shows a pattern of retreat westwards from more urbanised regions through the nineteenth century. Information on emigration likewise probably percolated westwards down the urban hierarchy of fairs and markets, through a network of travelling traders, beggars, and balladeers, much like the battered hats worn as status symbols by the poor peasantry in the west before the Famine:

> a generation out of fashion elsewhere, most had adorned more genteel heads before and had finally been picked up for pennies near the end of their half-life from the itinerant peddlers of second-hand goods . . . part of the flotsam and jetsam of the rag trade flowing from east to west circuitously seeking its lowest market where the final drops of profit could be wrung out.[3]

Thus questions of openness, accessibility and distance from centres of power or centres of change are important. Some of the descriptions of the poor communications in the west of Ireland in the nineteenth century dramatically illustrate the significance of location. John O'Donovan, working for the Ordnance Survey in west Donegal in the 1830s, had to journey through landscapes with neither roads nor bridges.[4] One of the most dramatic tests of the importance of location in the past was the differential local impact of famine relief measures and the tragic consequences of remoteness.

'Locality' in the past was a more bounded concept, more territorially restricted, than today. Local areas were more inward-looking, independent and self-sufficient, relying on their own indigenous resources whether physical, economic or social. Economic and settlement variations at local level in early modern Ireland often reflected the varying impact of locational factors, and areas of colonial plantation, areas of informal colonial infiltration, and areas of continuing Gaelic control illustrated the workings of distance, continuity, or openness. Unlike today when integration of localities is an everyday reality as well as an objective of EU policy, in past worlds peripherality of location could be of paramount significance for a place. Remote parishes in west Fermanagh or west Mayo up to the late nineteenth century were greatly reliant on their own limited and scarce resources. Only the small number of resident elite could rise above the limitations of location – contrast, for instance, the Big House and its imported stone facade with the peasant's vernacular house of local thatch and clay or stone. The nineteenth century, however, saw the beginnings of a great breakdown in distance as a factor influencing change and the sudden closeness, for example, of Carrickmacross (in Monaghan) to Liverpool, following the development of the steam packet and the railway, can be contrasted with the continuing remoteness of towns in west Mayo or Donegal.

IV

It is a truism that environmental factors in the past rated more highly in a local community's everyday life than in today's world of industrial agriculture and motorised landscapes. Human communities existed in a close symbiotic relationship with the physical environment of rocks, soils and plant cover. The rich Gaelic heritage of toponyms is a reflection of priorities in landscape perceptions in the distant past – *cor, drum, cluain,* for example, all were names with significance for landuse potential. Human settlement, therefore, was intimately bound up with quality of environment. By the time the various waves of colonists had arrived in Ireland, whether in the twelfth or sixteenth centuries, earlier occupants had to a great extent identified land-use potential, and Norman or Tudor or Stuart planters could fairly readily cherry-pick Gaelic or monastic pastures and granges.

During the sixteenth and seventeenth centuries, surveys were undertaken to establish the extent and nature of the environmental resources available for settlement and development in Ireland. Inventories of landscape potential reflected colonial intent and, as Raymond Gillespie points out for east Ulster in the late sixteenth century, data on agricultural land, fisheries and woods were assiduously collected as a preliminary to a programme of settlement and plantation. William Smith's survey of the barony of Farney in south Monaghan for the earl of Essex in 1611 listed 1,458 acres of woods, 336 acres of bog, and good turbary, fourteen large lakes full of pike and eels, limestone for building and a stream suitable for an eighteen-foot mill wheel at Carrickmacross.[5] Many surveys of the seventeenth century, especially the Civil Survey of 1654, endeavoured with some success to outline land quality, separating arable from wasteland. For example, in the barony of Salt, according to the Civil Survey for Kildare:

> the soyle is generally moist and specially the meadoe grounds pastures and underwoods. The arrable land in ye said Barony being well manured will yield good corne. The south part is somewhat hilly and mountainous but is held to be good pasture for cattle. . .[6]

Later the eighteenth-century preoccupation with 'improvements' is echoed in the Rev. William Henry's assessment of west Fermanagh in 1739:

> not much of it is profitable for tillage, the cold clay lying so near the surface in most places that scarce any manure will meliorate it. Sand and lime are found the most effectual marle had been often tried but in vain. Besides the exceeding dampness of the air prevents corn from ripening till late in the season by which means it is often destroyed. The last of the harvest is often out till the middle of October.[7]

Griffith's Valuation in the middle of the nineteenth century was the ultimate effort by central government to catalogue the land and property of Ireland for taxation purposes, and was one of a number of examples of Victorian obsession with data accumulation. It records and values the environmental resources of Ireland at the end of more than two centuries of reclamation and husbandry of varying intensities in all the localities of Ireland.

In this age of the deregulation of economies, it is possible to apply the principle of comparative advantage retrospectively to consider the links between local social and economic conditions and environments in the past.

In a situation of little or no centralised intervention in local economies, as was the case for most localities up to the nineteenth century, each district strove to reach its maximum potential according to its physical endowment. Areas poor in natural resources, such as good soils or favourable climatic conditions, were under-developed and impoverished in comparison with more richly endowed regions. Thus parishes in the west of Ireland since the seventeenth century developed largely as nurturing areas for young cattle which were moved eastwards to the fatlands and ports. Alternatively, they participated in the early spinning stages in domestic textile processing, feeding their output eastwards into the yarn markets. As the agricultural and cottage industry came under pressure in the early nineteenth century, western parishes also became nurturing areas for growing numbers of young people who the local economy could not absorb and who had to migrate eastwards in search of work in Ireland or beyond. In this colonial-type setting, therefore, a perverse kind of environmental logic attached to the marginal lands of Ireland where an escalating imbalance between labour and economic resources – population and land – had developed by the early 1800s. Poverty, squatting and squalor were associated with boglands and badlands throughout the island by the 1840s.

V

Environmental conditions merge imperceptibly into economic processes of change in the landscape, macro economic forces operating through microprocesses at local level. For example, the repercussions of colonialism, mercantilism or industrial capitalism – articulated through state legislation like the Act of Settlement, Cattle Acts, Navigation Acts and Factory Acts – were filtered into the rural recesses of the landscape, the bogs and meadowlands, the river valleys and mountainsides.

As an aid to understanding the making of the Irish landscape and the myriad localities which comprised it, the landed estates system represents a useful framework. Although the landowning class was by no means homogeneous, as a fairly universal system which evolved throughout the island, it is a sort of territorial template with which to interpret the transforming impact of macro-economic processes in local landscapes. Undoubtedly, at local level important sectors of the community fell outside the structure of the estates and in some areas the estates were so ephemeral as to be almost non-existent, yet their structure, clear or opaque, can be used to interpret negative or positive influences on change. In the idealised model, the estate management responded to wider economic processes by mustering its resources and matching its rents to prices. The rent-paying tenants responded by 'developing' the landscape, frequently under the watchful eye of the landlord or his agent, resulting perhaps in manifestations of the so-called 'age of improvement' at local level. Alternatively, in locations where estates had a low profile, tenant inputs to the landscape were more uncoordinated and perhaps even anarchic, but no less significant for that. The nature of the evidence probably provides an unrepresentative sample of landscape evolution on the centralised, managed estates. In Tipperary, for example, Smyth was able to identify a series of stages in the development of the landscape of the Shanbally estate: a period of initiation (1730-1775), when the skeletal framework of the modern landscape emerged; a period of elaboration up to 1815 which represented the peak phase of landowner investment and modification of the landscape and a period of reorientation after 1815, when the estate system had to adjust not only to radical changes in the agricultural economy but a long decline in the privileges of ascendancy.[8] More effort should probably be made to throw light on the processes operating on the poorly managed, absentee or non-resident properties where large rundale settlements represented forms of tenant control of landscape change. In the Bath estate in south Monaghan, many of the townlands were held jointly under middlemen tenants by subtenants living in house clusters in 1777. Subsequently, however, the estate broke up these clusters when the land was re-let to the occupiers.[9]

VI

One of the by-products of Ireland's peripherality and relative poverty in a European context has been the survival of a significant level of local diversity in life and culture. Until recently this was negatively perceived as parochialism and backwardness. The tourism industry today, however, unashamedly exploits the survival of local cultural diversity in Ireland. The cultural diversity in music is especially celebrated today, and increasingly local places are celebrating their local distinctiveness in buildings and heritage.[10]

Estyn Evans' *Irish Heritage*, first published in 1942, established an agenda which is only at this stage coming to be widely appreciated, and the popularity of the Evans-inspired Ulster Folk and Transport Museum, and other similar folk history parks in Ireland which celebrate the integrity of local landscape, is a measure of this. The chapters in Evans' book bring out the important, if taken-for-granted, elements in local cultural landscapes: woodlands, fields, fences and gates; village and booley; the Irish peasant house; interior of the house – fireside and food; farm buildings; carts and roads; the bog; the sea-shore; festivals and fairs; the country town; customs and

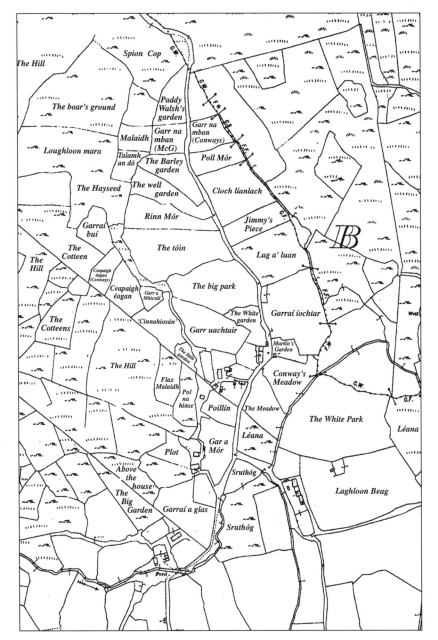

Figure 2: Field names in Loughloon, Co. Mayo.

beliefs.[11] The Irish Folklore Commission, later the Department of Irish Folklore in University College, Dublin, has been for seventy years quietly assembling an enormous data collection on all aspects of Irish local community culture and some ways of using this are suggested by Linda May Ballard's essay below.

The process of subdivision and naming local places and territories must be among some of the most pervasive aspects in the building of landscapes in the past. Past landscape order and organisation, for example, are reflected in house, farmyard, 'street', fields, farmholding, townland and parish. These represent sequences in the creation of places by the people who occupied these locales in the past and collectively they contribute to the differences in texture of landscape from one place to another. The sense of place is a cultural and emotional amalgam of the familiar 'feel' and experience of the shapes, curves and angles of farmyard, byre, headland, townland and hill. A spatial step upwards from the farm are the townlands, units of supreme importance in the Irish cultural landscape.[12] They have been cartographically recorded for posterity in shape and name from the seventeenth century and form important building blocks in attempts to understand the morphology of the local landscape. Whatever about the landed estate as a unit of landscape interpretation, the townland has been the container within which landholding and landscape changes have waxed and waned for centuries as W. H. Crawford's essay below suggests. The parish has also represented the community's territorial expression – a place of neighbours, kin, marriage alliances and community solidarity. There is evidence of discontinuity in parish settlement patterns following the Reformation, and the eighteenth-century re-emergence of Catholic parish centres is reflected in hundreds of lonely stranded graveyards and ivy-clad church ruins in the middle of fields in many countrysides. In Protestant-planted Ulster regions, the older units established in the Gaelic period seem to have largely survived for the Protestant and Catholic populations through to the present.[13]

The minute naming of places and farmscapes radiating out from the farmhouse is a reflection of the more crowded and local landscapes of the past, as well as a memorial to those past generations who manhandled the rocks and clay of their home places. Unfortunately, most of the intimate local names are now forgotten in emptier and tractored landscapes: many of the fields which were given homely names with local significance have themselves been removed, and the owners of the land have no need or use for such local labelling. Many of the names recorded in this century are emblematic of a recent past when Irish was a familiar and living language in places where it is now long forgotten. In one north Monaghan parish, for example, there were

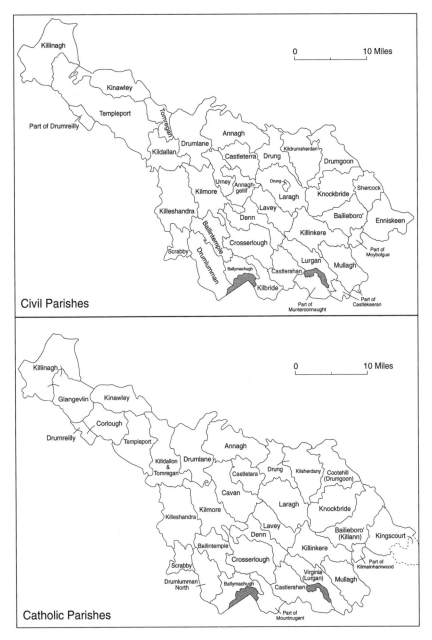

Figure 3: Civil and Catholic parishes in the diocese of Clogher.

fields in the early twentieth century with names like *Páirc tóin na mbó, Garrdha na gcrann, Garrdha na heorna, Páirc éadain, Páirc an fhéir, Poll na Fola, An Spinnc, Poll na steall, Garrdha na bplandaí*. In another parish in the middle of Monaghan, most of the names were in English, or variants of forgotten Irish – the smoothing iron, the footstick field, the black garden, the carrycar, the parawhack, the baychin, glenmore, the cowan, the rassan.[14]

The townland names outside the area of Anglo–Norman manorial settlement reflect a Gaelic past which placed a high priority on pastoral agricultural land potential. John O'Donovan speculated in the 1830s that it is possible that many of the names of units of great territorial antiquity might be relatively recent, suggesting, for example, that names like Lisnagore, Lisnalee or Rakeeragh in the Monaghan parish of Aghnamullen, are probably modern associations (with goats, calves and sheep) applied to local ring forts. Some of the most interesting cultural transitions in landscapes occur across the old frontiers around the Pale, where there are sometimes quite abrupt changes from the English prefixes *castle, court, grange, grove* and the ubiquitous suffix *-town* to the overwhelmingly Gaelic names of south Ulster and the west midlands.[15]

In sharp contrast to the workaday folk landscapes were the exotically named landscapes of leisure of the eighteenth–century ascendancy and landowning class. The Romantic Movement especially resulted in fanciful, often 'frenchified' names such as Belle Field, Beaulieu, Belvedere, Dolly Mount (later Delamont, in county Down), Mount Tally-Ho (later Montalto also in Down) and places called after wives or daughters such as Bessmount, Annesborough or Bettyford.[16] Many of these demesne landscapes came equipped with 'pleasure grounds', follies, ornamental ruins like the Gothick arch in Belvedere county Westmeath, artificial lakes, evocations in the landscape of very different lifestyles and cultural priorities to those of the local population.

VII

Among the most important social influences in the making of the landscape was the population. The most significant modifications of the landscape were made during the most crowded period in the history of the Irish countryside. Half a million kilometres of hedges were laid down during the century before the Famine. Rural population density was connected with the farm structure, in which the day-to-day mechanics of rural landscape change were undertaken. Small farms had small fields, most dramatically reflected in the gardens of Connemara. The highest population density was associated inevitably with the smallest farms: one square mile of five- to ten-acre farms in 1841 would have contained up to one hundred farmhouses, each with perhaps up to six occupants. This would have characterised much of south Ulster or parts of west Mayo. Contrast this with the comparatively empty landscapes of most of Kildare and Meath where a square mile might have been divided into farms between fifty and one hundred acres comprising ten or a dozen farmhouses. Together with perhaps a handful of labourer cabins this would amount to little more than fifty people.

Population experience is therefore a useful surrogate indicator of landscape experience, and the accretion and augmentation of the pre-Famine period of population expansion was matched by a process of dereliction and landscape contraction which followed decades of continuous population decline. Kevin Whelan graphically describes this process in west Mayo:

> The tenacious combination of potato and lazy bed had allowed cultivation to spread into even the most unpropitious locations. The tide of population which flowed into these valleys and up the hillsides ebbed rapidly during and after the Famine and today these withered scars on the landscape, quilted under heather and bracken, compose their own oblique requiem to the crowded generations of pre-famine Ireland. . . eight million people who had by 1841 surged into every conceivable nook and cranny.[17]

The most marginal landscapes were abandoned first as the line of settlement retreated progressively downhill. Due to the peculiarity of demographic decline, where migration especially was a slow generationally-selective process, there was a time-lag between abandonment of land and population decline. Only during crises like the Famine were houses and farms abandoned suddenly, though John Healy documented hurried departures from east Mayo in the bleak years of the 1950s. The norm was a gradual imperceptible running-down of landscape. First one house, then another closed, with lanes, drains and hedgerows gradually becoming derelict and overgrown.

Another important aspect of social change in local landscapes relates to landholding. To what extent did peasant proprietorship, as it has been called, affect landscape change? Following the late nineteenth-century Land Acts, the farmers had achieved the ultimate stake in the landscape – ownership of the land, masters inside their own fences. Did removal of the pressure of gale days change their relationship with the landscape? Raymond Crotty thought it did, and for the worse.[18] Farm consolidation went hand-in-hand with rural population decline, but as with settlement contraction, there was no immediate correspondence between them. A consequence of owner occupiership was land immobility: a great many small holdings in poorer emigration-prone regions of the west continued in the possession of families long after they had emigrated. In the 1950s and 1960s it was possible to pick out these unworked and unoccupied farms with their rush-infested fieldscapes. It was also sometimes possible to identify in the landscapes of the north-west another by-product of rural social change from the post-Famine decades. This was the bachelor farm, a demographic consequence of postponed marriage and permanent celibacy in circumstances of rural poverty, where there was neither the incentive of rent nor the motivation of family to maintain the landscape legacy of the farm.

VIII

Enlarged or diminished, embellished or purified, lengthened or abbreviated, the past becomes more and more a foreign country, yet also increasingly tinged with present colours.[19]

The lesson today is that there is a constant revision of the past, re-interpretations arising from or fitting into the ideologies of the present day. The very designation of 'interpretative centre' implies the processing and packaging of versions of the past, a past which is more and more separated from the people today. Indeed the peculiar needs of tourism result in a process of commodification which is characterised by distinctive social constructions of landscapes and societies in the past, which may be represented, for example, as places of happiness, wholesomeness and authenticity, symbolised by sparkling thatched cottages or gentrified Georgian mansions. Local history, perhaps, offers greater scope to keep in touch with the past, *our* past which belongs to us rather than being a foreign place. It is part of the story and the memory of the people who lived in a very familiar place. The geographical reality of the local past, therefore, is an important key to maintaining contact with the past of the local place and, in one way, knowing its past in this way deepens the knowledge and understanding of the local landscape.

It might appear, however, that the story of the landscape (the geography) is less amenable to ideological distortion than the story of events (the history): the landscape cannot be blamed for some of the happenings in it in the past! But, as the preceding discussion has shown, the landscape story is also a layered and complex one. The cultural geographer Meinig has said that 'any landscape is composed not only of what lies before our eyes but also what lies in our heads'.[20] The processes which went into the making of the landscape are open to interpretation in different ways by different people. At local level, for example, the farmer's and the labourer's perspectives on their landscapes may be quite different. Similarly it is interesting to consider how the landowning ascendancy perceived their landscapes from their vantage of houses and demesnes: in the pre-Famine period in the works of Maria Edgeworth, for example; in the late nineteenth century in the works of Somerville and Ross; in the 1930s in the writings of Elizabeth Bowen perhaps; and more recently, in the writings of Molly Keane or the views of Desmond Leslie of Glaslough or Lord Altamont in Westport. At local level of course, their views and their landscapes and what they symbolise are still regarded with suspicion by sections of the community. The local landscape, therefore, is a text that is open to a variety of interpretations.

IX

Much of the foregoing discussion of approaches to studying the historical geography of local areas relies on a variety of sources which are particularly used by the geographer, such as maps and surveys, sources with a strong territorial dimension, particularly ones which allow cross sections in time, as well as field surveys and other material which help illuminate landscape and place. Art and literature, for example, can also provide valuable insights to the sense of place and the distinctive character of local landscapes.

It is important to understand the meaning of maps because on this will hang understanding of their limitations and uses. Maps are essentially representations of part of the earth's surface, in which symbols are used to indicate the presence, extent and shape of different items (such as buildings) or characteristics (such as altitude or environmental quality) in the landscape. There are two other significant characteristics of maps: as symbolic representations maps can only show selections or parts of the landscape reality, and related to this, the area depicted is a scaled down version of reality. Maps, like writing and language, are an important symbolic part of living and so it is appropriate that they should form part of local studies. We use maps almost unconsciously, because we live territorially. Our place and our behaviour is spatial and so one of our basic tools of communication should be some form of representation of this spatial dimension to our lives – today and in the past.

Maps can be useful firstly as documents or sources of data in themselves and, secondly, as a means of presenting data in a local area study. As data sources, maps in Ireland reflect the distinctive nature of the Irish past: the struggle for the land of Ireland whether as a colonial prize by settlers, as a family possession by an elite or as a rented peasant holding has meant that the land, its boundaries and other cadastral features are fairly well recorded and care-

fully preserved locally. Other aspects of the landscape, such as its suite of settlement and communications net are only incidentally recorded before the
Ordnance Survey of the nineteenth century.

As sources of data of use to the local historian, topographic and administrative maps have different potential uses. In Ireland there is a range of map
documents which have considerable topographical use and which have been
comprehensively studied and catalogued by John Andrews.[21] Paul
Ferguson's *Irish Map History* is a good guide to where to begin looking
although new maps are being discovered fairly regularly.[22] Irish maps begin
with the great state-sponsored land mapping surveys which accompanied the
various plantation schemes of the late sixteenth and seventeenth centuries,
for instance, the maps of the Ulster Plantation and the Down Survey.[23]

With the consolidation and economic development of estates in the eighteenth century came a range of privately commissioned estate surveys. These
date mainly from the middle of the eighteenth century. The greatest expo-
nents of this craft were John Rocque, who came over to Ireland in 1754 to
make a map of Dublin and set up a surveying business there with his son-in-
law Bernard Scalé. There are many more inferior estate maps which are often
useful for the local detail they provide. Estate maps with other estate papers
provide only a patchy coverage, with a concentration obviously on the larger
and better-managed properties.

Just as the surveying profession was coming into its own in producing
comprehensive maps of estates by the early nineteenth century, the state
intervened. In response to the growing land and population problem and the
need to produce an equitable Poor Law land tax, the government established
the Ordnance Survey which began in the 1830s to produce the most comprehensive cartographic survey of the landscape for the first time. The six-
inch survey, which fortunately predated the great Famine and the resulting
widescale transformation of many local landscapes, remains as an important
monument to pre-Famine landscape studies. The one-inch scale and the
town plans are other useful sources for the later nineteenth-century landscapes.[24]

Apart from topographic information, maps also provide important information on the territorial organisation of the landscape, especially as it is
organised into administrative and territorial structures. The Townland Index
map is one of the most useful maps produced. It originated as an index to the
six-inch survey and at this stage has become a poorly reproduced and largely
obsolete map in the Republic, although it is an important and intimate document of the shape of the countryside, particularly the network of townlands. For the local historian these administrative units are important

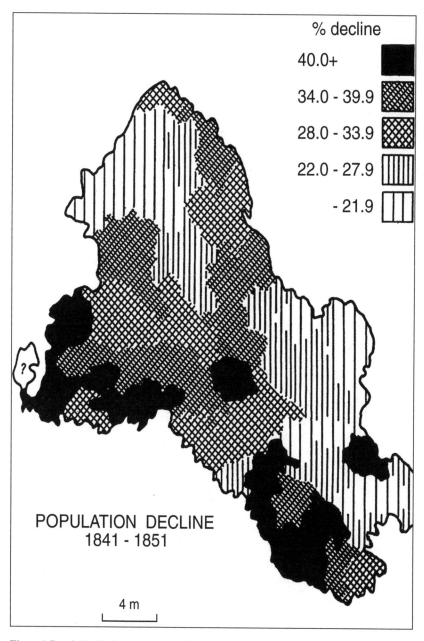

% decline

40.0+

34.0 - 39.9

28.0 - 33.9

22.0 - 27.9

- 21.9

POPULATION DECLINE
1841 - 1851

4 m

Figure 4: Population decline by electoral division, county Monaghan.

information sources and important containers of data. This is especially true of the nineteenth and to a lesser extent the eighteenth century: data on a range of subjects were collected on a townland, parish, barony or Rural District basis and can be retrieved in this form.

The other principal use of maps is as a means of presenting data. Though cartographic representation is especially associated with geographers, it is a useful means of illustrating spatial aspects of a study. These kinds of maps are distinguished by their concentration on a restricted and focused theme, unlike the topographical maps which include a broad range of information. Thematic maps in this sense can be qualitatively or quantitatively descriptive. They may be locational or non-numeric (showing the location of points or patterns) or numeric (showing ranges or intensities of values over an area). In most cases, the type of map presentation will be dictated by the requirements of the study. Locational maps may be generalised versions of data obtained from topographical maps such as, for example, the road network extracted from a nineteenth-century Ordnance Survey map, or data collected in the field such as the distribution of ring forts. Quantitative-type maps take data from another documentary source such as the census, and present them often in administrative divisions, for example, population density by Electoral Divisions. Shadings (or choropleths) are used to distinguish one value in one area from another as in the case of population change (figure four).

Apart from maps, the most popular sources which have been widely used by historical geographers have been those which have assembled recorded data comprehensively by territorial unit. When available, these are especially useful in constructing cross-sectional profiles of landscapes. Examples which have been used to throw light on the evolution of landholding and landownership have been the mid seventeenth-century Civil Survey and the Books of Survey and Distribution, as well as the Tithe Applotment Books and Griffith's Valuation of the nineteenth century. Geographers have been especially interested in the Valuation and the manuscript cancellation books in the Valuation Office and in the Public Record Office of Northern Ireland for the light they cast on post-Famine landholding and population experience at local level. T. W. Freeman studied nineteenth-century population patterns in Ireland by using the detailed census reports from 1841, and he produced one of the most comprehensive maps of rural population density in Ireland for 1841.[25] The household enumeration forms from the 1901 and 1911 censuses have also proven extremely popular as sources for local population dynamics. These are among the assets of the local historian in Ireland which help to counter some of the negative consequences of the destruction of so many documents in 1922. In Northern Ireland, Estyn Evans established

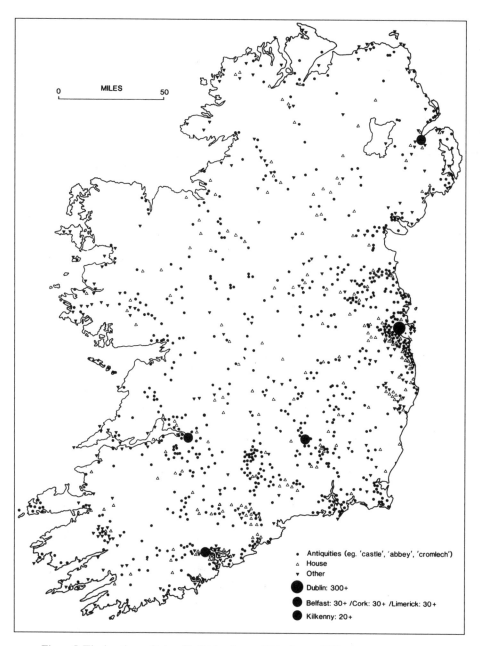

MILES

0   50

Antiquities (eg. 'castle', 'abbey', 'cromlech')
△ House
▼ Other
● Dublin: 300+
● Belfast: 30+ /Cork: 30+ /Limerick: 30+
● Kilkenny: 20+

Figure 5: The locations of 'views' in Irish prints published up to 1850.

an abiding interest in the rural cultural landscape, especially rural settlement and buildings, based on a sound field survey tradition. Evans and his successors have mapped ring fort and rural settlement patterns throughout Ireland, which have recently been updated and supplemented by the extensive field surveys of the Office of Public Works in the Republic and the Archaeological Survey of Northern Ireland.

Artistic sources such as paintings, photographs and literature often contain important representations of landscapes in the past. However, while landscape paintings, for example, might seem at first sight to be of obvious value in depicting what a landscape looked like in the past, one needs to be alert to the special nature of these sources and the subjectivity and biases of the painter or recorder. 'Rose-tinted imagery' frequently characterised these depictions of landscape and many places were painted in a manner which would please a client or sell at an exhibition.[26] In addition, like estate maps, landscape art is a fragmentary and patchy source, with some types of area or landscape proving more popular than others. Urban fringe areas, demesnes and parklands and popular tourist areas in the eighteenth century are often especially rich in these views (figure five). Similarly, photograph collections are also often selective, with towns and villages, for example, being more popular than many open countrysides.

Literature such as novels and poetry also often offer uniquely interesting perspectives on landscapes and countrysides in the past as Myrtle Hill shows below. These include formal works of creative literature such as Kickham's *Knocknagow* and Edgeworth's *Castle Rackrent* or Sam Hanna Bell's *December Bride*, all of which in various ways capture the ambience and sense of place of the regions in which they are located. Indeed novels about the past written in the present are often useful sources, so powerful is the insight of the artist in many cases. An examples of this genre would be J. G. Farrell's *Troubles*. The poetry of Yeats, Kavanagh, Heaney, MacNeice and many others offer important reflections on their local landscapes to the extent that these regions are frequently identified with the names of their distinguished authors: Yeats Country, Kavanagh Country, Goldsmith Country for example.

Knowing one's place, its landscape and social identity, is an increasingly respectable preoccupation today, in great contrast with thirty or more years ago when such interests were seen as parochial, backward and irrelevant. Nowadays, cherishing local cultural distinctiveness is a valid political objective, and thanks to tourism, it has a viable economic potential.

Local studies represent the academic response to these dawning realities. Ironically, one of the principal reasons for the growth in interest in local studies is probably the extent and speed of change in the last generation, a process of homogenisation and modernisation of society and economy which has obliterated or vastly simplified the complex geographies and histories of local places. Technology has resulted in a sort of spatial closure in life and landscape. The territorial structure of rural society in Ireland has been transformed from a highly complex localised framework. The hierarchy of localities, or pyramid of places where local was dominant – from house to yard, to field, farm, village, townland, to parish and beyond – has been inverted. Territorialisation, at local level reflected in an intimately detailed information field, has been simplified or abandoned. In many ways, life is now lived more intensely at a regional, national and international level than ever before. The ultimate expression of this process is reflected in e-mail and the World Wide Web: 'networking' at international rather than local levels.

Paralleling this abandonment of local worlds is a selective appropriation of these places and their pasts, especially by the city, where more and more of the policy-makers, as well as the consumers of landscape, now live. This is represented especially in the all-embracing needs of the tourism industry, which through heritage tourism, for example, commodifies and packages local cultural diversity and its stories and pasts to suit the transient fancies and fads of tourism. Local studies, therefore, have a responsibility and opportunity to recover and defend the integrity of the local community and landscape.

1. A. J. Brown and E. M. Burrows, *Regional economic problems* (London, 1977), p. 49.
2. Robert Scally, *The end of hidden Ireland: rebellion, famine and emigration* (Oxford, 1995), chapter 7.
3. Scally, *End of hidden Ireland*, p. 32.
4. John O'Donovan, Ordnance Survey Letters, Co. Donegal (typescript).
5. Raymond Gillespie, *Colonial Ulster: the settlement of east Ulster 1600-41* (Cork, 1985) Ch. 1; Longleat House, Irish papers 'A Booke of Survey of fferney & Clancarvill in the Kingdom of Ireland 1612. William Smith'.
6. R. C. Simington (ed.), *The civil survey, 1654-6, vii Kildare* (10 vols, Dublin, 1931-61), p. 3.
7. W. Henry, 'Towards a topographical history of the Counties Sligo, Donegal. Fermanagh and Lough Erne', Public Record Office of Northern Ireland, D 1739.
8. W. J. Smyth, 'Estate records and the making of the Irish landscape: an example from county Tipperary' in *Irish Geography* ix (1976), pp. 29-48.
9. See P. J. Duffy, *Landscapes of south Ulster: a parish atlas of the diocese of Clogher* (Belfast, 1993), p. 21.

10. U. Kockel (ed.), *Culture, tourism and development: the case of Ireland* (Liverpool, 1994).
11. E. E. Evans, *Irish heritage: The landscape, the people and their work* (Dundalk, 1942).
12. See J. H. Andrews, 'Topography: territorial divisions' in *Encyclopaedia of Ireland* (London, 1968), pp. 142–47.
13. Duffy, *Landscapes of south Ulster*, Introduction.
14. From the Schools Collection, Irish Folklore Commission. See also P. O'Flanagan and S. Ó. Cáthain, *The living landscape: Kilgalligan, county Mayo* (Dublin, 1975).
15. T. Jones Hughes, 'Town and Baile in Irish placenames' in Nicholas Stephens and Robert Glascock (eds), *Irish Geographical Studies* (Belfast, 1970), pp. 244–58.
16. Robert T. Campbell, 'A retrospective view of Irish country houses and villas in the rural and urban environment', PhD thesis, Queen's University of Belfast, 1996, p. 560.
17. Kevin Whelan, 'The Famine and post-Famine adjustment' in William Nolan (ed.), *The shaping of Ireland* (Dublin, 1986), p. 151.
18. Raymond Crotty, *Irish agricultural production* (Cork, 1966).
19. David Lowenthal, *The past is a foreign country* (Cambridge, 1985), p. 362; see also John Urry, *The tourist gaze* (London, 1990), chapter 6.
20. D. W. Meinig, 'The beholding eye' in D. W. Meinig et al. (eds), *The interpretation of ordinary landscapes* (Oxford, 1979), p. 34.
21. J. H. Andrews, *A paper landscape:the Ordnance Survey in nineteenth century Ireland* (Oxford, 1975); J. H. Andrews *Plantation acres* (Belfast, 1985).
22. Paul Ferguson, *Irish map history: A select bibliography 1850–1983* (Dublin, 1983).
23. See William Nolan, *Tracing the past* (Dublin, 1982).
24. See J. H. Andrews, *History in the Ordnance map: an introduction for Irish readers* (Dublin, 1974).
25. T. W. Freeman, *Pre-famine Ireland* (Manchester, 1957); reprinted in Whelan, 'The Famine and post-Famine adjustment', p. 153.
26. P. J. Duffy, 'The changing rural landscape 1750-1850: pictorial evidence' in Raymond Gillespie and B. P. Kennedy (eds), *Ireland: art into history* (Dublin, 1994).

THE FOLKLORIST AND LOCAL HISTORY

Linda May Ballard

There is a school of thought, rather old-fashioned nowadays, which considers folklore to be anathema to the historian. According to this approach, folklore may at best be dismissed because it deals in absurd notions set in an era which fails to allow for any sense of the passage of time. At worst, folklore may be despised for its mutability, its capacity constantly to reorder and reconstruct the past, untrammelled as it is by any fixed terms of reference. Put as crudely as this, it is easy to argue the opposite case in favour of folklore. It is also necessary to acknowledge the historian's justification in regarding folklore with a certain amount of suspicion.

Folklore is mutable. Part of its nature is its capacity to be reordered. To understand this is to come to a better awareness of its nature and, therefore, to appreciate its strengths. Like any source, folklore should be weighed and considered, and above all it should not be bent to inappropriate or impossible ends. The first duty of a folklorist who wishes to illuminate any aspect of local history is to avoid the temptation to present the past as if this were a monolithic entity. 'Once upon a time. . .' or 'Fadó, fadó' may do very well as the introduction to a fairy tale, but provides little service to those of us who try to understand or appreciate the nature of experience in the past. Folklore is among the best, and perhaps it is the best, of resources available to us for this purpose, but like all sources, it needs a modicum of appreciation, understanding and interpretation if this is to be extracted from it. We might call this the objective approach to the subject.

As well as being a product, folklore is a process by which one may be placed in relation to the past. Subjectively, the hearer of (for example) a story may become part of a chain by which past knowledge is made available in the present and for the future. In this sense, the 'fadó, fadó,' style of presentation retains some validity and may, therefore, be of historical value. The potential for the folklorist also to be a tradition bearer is one matter. The capacity of folklore to offer a useful resource to the historian is another, much broader issue.

The word 'folklore' itself embraces a broad canon, subsuming as it does many different genres. It may be useful to look at certain types of narrative, and to consider their potential historical value. The first example is of a 'personal experience' narrative, someone telling a story which directly relates an individual experience:

> . . . my father was a great man for teaching us history by taking us to the places and telling us the story of them. We had just heard, when we were small children, about the Famine, and when we asked him about it he took us to see two old men living side by side on tiny farms – this was in the early days of this century and I was a small child, and they were very old men . . . the families decided the farms would only support one man, and that the rest of the family would have to emigrate . . . They all walked to Dublin, taking two days. They went by way of Clonee, which is just on the border of Meath and Dublin, and they lit a bonfire there and sat round it and sang the whole night to keep their spirits up. They sang ballads, he said, and any song that anyone could raise . . . and they kept the fire going until daylight, nobody slept, and then they walked down to the Dublin Quays where there was always a sailing ship going to America. They hadn't booked any tickets, but they all got on board anyway, and the two families went on board and sailed, he thought, that night.
>
> He and the other man walked back, but he said that when they got to Clonee they just kicked the ashes of the bonfire, but they didn't stop, they had no heart to sit or to rest, and they had nothing more to eat, anyway. So they went back to the farm and got there on the night of the next day, and he said, 'And we never left the farm since.' I said, 'Did neither of you marry?' And he said, 'There was no money to raise a family on either farm'. And they just lived on, each on his own wee farm . . .
>
> I asked him what was the kind of farm, and he said they'd had a cow at first on each farm, or maybe two, but they'd to sell the cows, and when the potatoes failed, they'd nothing, they had no form of culture that they knew on the farm but the grazing of the cow, and the potato field. And when the potatoes failed for the third time, there was nothing. They had a few hens, that was all. I said, 'And what about your family in America, did they make good there?' He said, 'I don't know.' I said, 'Did you never hear from them?' He said, 'Either they died of the fever on the way or before they ever got there, but we never heard another word of any of them.' And I said, 'Would there not have been someone to write to you?' And he said, 'Child dear with the education in those days, none of us could read or write.'[1]

Strictly speaking, this is a personal experience narrative at second hand, since we are most likely to be concerned with the information this story provides about the experience of the Famine. The account is an excellent example of the potential of oral history. It extends our knowledge by providing in great detail an intimation of the reality of living through the actuality of the Famine years, transmitted at only one remove across the years from the 1840s to 1981, when the account was recorded on tape. It is easy to lose sight of the teller's introductory remark which explains how she came to be in such a situation, and which makes the story her own.

Oral history, often directly expressed from personal experience, can be a very important source for the study of social history. Consider the implications of the following account, recorded in 1983 and referring to the 1940s:

Inf. If you had heard somebody saying some girl had a wee child, that was like a crime, wasn't it? That was a crime. God bless us.

L.B. That didn't happen?

Inf. That would have been a disgrace.

L.B. If that did happen, would it have been kept a big secret, then?

Inf. Sure it did . . . but thank God I never heard nothing like. I heard about one girl, right enough. I think she'd tried to do away with, or something, they were talking about her. I don't know what happened. She didn't want nobody to know about it.

L.B. And she tried to do away with the baby?

Inf. Tried to do away with the child.

L.B. Before it was born, or . . .?

Inf. After it was born. She was living in, wasn't married, now, lived across the Grosvenor Road in somebody's house. She left her own house, do you see? Suppose . . .

L.B. She was thrown out, like, or . . .?

Inf. Before the people would get to know about it. Now, I worked with a woman, Mary. I suppose she's living. I don't know whether she's living or dead, now. Me and her was very great. The time of the evacuees, she was evacueed to up the country, to some big country place, her and the childer. The time the war was on.

L.B. The second war, was this?

Inf. The blitz. And Mary was telling me she was in this house. I forget the name of the wee place it was in, now, but me and her was very, very great in work. She says to me one day, she says, 'Maggie, I had a visitor,' she says. 'Do you mind I told you, away, the place she stayed in. I can't mind it now, up the country, but they were very good to her and the childer. She says, 'The girl come down, to me,' she says, 'and, eh, she wants to stay with me . . . She's expecting a baby, and nobody up there knows. But she says she doesn't want the baby. She wants to know if she has it, [do I] know anybody would adopt it?' See? So we worked, a girl worked with us. . . her mother had already reared a wee girl, you know? Lovely wee girl, and I says, eh, 'Well if she had the wee child, maybe. . .I'll ask. . .would her mother take it. But we have to wait,' I says, 'to see will the child be living or dead.' Child not born yet, do you see? Well, she stayed with Mary. Mary lived up in Ardoyne, now. She stayed with Mary, anyway, to she took bad and she was up in the City Hospital. I think, the Jubilee was built then, I think, or was it? I couldn't tell you. But that's where the child was born, anyway.

So Mary went up to see her, and Mary says, 'She's getting out on such a day, and I've to go up for her,' she says, 'and I'll bring her round.' Now, we asked – I asked – I says, 'Maggie, Mary knows a girl, and she's a wee baby, and she doesn't want to go home, and she belongs to up the country. Do you think would, your mother take it?' Now – her mother reared a big family, Mrs — did, a big family. So Maggie had already asked her mother, and the mother says, 'I'll see what . . . I'll let her come down till I see her and the child when she has it.' Like, says she, 'She has the baby, but she's not out of the hospital yet.' Maggie had told her mother all that.

But anyway, that day Mary went up for her, to take her out. Mary didn't get into work. They took her home, out of the hospital, she brought her round to me. And my man was sitting there. Lord rest his soul but he went out and stood at the door. And eh, the child was lovely. Oh, you wanted to see it, lovely child, and I says to her, 'Would you not keep it?' I says, 'Aw, he's lovely.' A wee boy, now. No, it was a wee girl, sandy haired, she says. 'Oh no,' she says, 'I want rid of it.' That hurt me, to hear her saying that, like. And I says, 'Well,' I told Mary then, I told Mary, where to go up to where Mrs — lived, with the child, I left her up — Street, do you see? Wasn't too far from where I lived. So that woman took the child. Kept it. And Mary used to say to me, after she went away back home. She never hardly sent a scrape, never sent a ha'penny down. And I said, 'Mrs — is very . . . She should write her a letter. Sending nothing . . . So, one day, a letter come, with money in it. And after that, she never got . . . Aw that big girl, that child's married now long ago . . .

L.B. And she just did that . . . out of kindness, like, she took those children and reared them?

Inf. Yes. Yes.

L.B. And got nothing for it, just . . .?

Inf. No. But the first one, she was looked . . . she was well paid for it, because they had a wee bit of business, do you see, the girl that . . . that had the child. And she was the picture of her mother, but, I could still see them faces yet. I . . . I . . . going up to work every meal hour I seen them outside the door, do you see — Street School was at that corner, and our house was on the other side from it. But she was good to them, the two childer. But the wee red-haired one, that was the country girl's one . . . well, Mary thought it, she said her mother, were great people, too. For she said they were good to her and her . . . that's why she took her in, because when they were evacuated, they were very, very good to her, and her childer. But I'm sure her mother was bound to know about her.

Well, it seems she told Mary in a letter, then, she wrote her a letter, and whoever she had the child to, then he was going to marry her. Then, you see, people up there didn't know there was anything wrong with her. See now?

L.B. So she couldn't take the child back, then?

Inf. No, no. Didn't want it back, then. Said, she didn't want it. Sat in my house and said it, she didn't want it.[2]

Secondary to the main point, the account illustrates the potential strength of personal ties first made as a result of wartime evacuation, hints at the possibility of infanticide (rather than abortion), and shows the power of attitudes to illegitimacy prevalent less than half a century ago. Its primary value is, of course, for the insight it supplies into mechanisms by which adoption might operate, a matter for which information is not always readily available, particularly in an era not long past.

It is not particularly surprising that accounts like this have the potential to provide information about the past, since they are straightforward descriptions of that past. We may have concerns about reliability, but are there strong reasons for preferring written autobiography to an oral description? Is the oral account less likely to be accurate than the diary or newspaper? Oral material may be subjected to various tests and checks. It may be compared, for example, with itself, with related oral material, or with material drawn from written sources. It is fortuitous that sources exist which enable just such a comparison to be made in the case of this example, a ballad relating to events which took place in July, 1846, and which was recorded in 1978:

On the thirteenth of July, we remember that day,
We met at the Cock in splendid array,
We met at the Cock, where the grog it went round,
And then we marched off unto Seaforde town.

We marched up through Drumaughlis more glorious to be seen,
It was there we were treated by David 'the king',
He treated us all just as we passed by,
And then led before us unto Annacloy.

When we got there, we were joined by some more,
There was Killyleagh, Creavy, Crossgar and Kilmore,
Amongst the 'True Blues' there was none to compare
To young John McRoberts who rode a grey mare.

We loaded our pistols without fear or dread
And he rode before us unto the Buck's Head
And when we got there some Threshers did stand
So we fired our pistols and they ran every man.

When we landed in Seaforde a glorious sight there was seen
of William III and Victoria the Queen
On every corner an arch I record
Got up there by the order of his honour Major Forde.

We got our refreshments, we never did yield
When called by our numbers we marched to the Field
On the platform erected the Rev. Boyd he did stand
He read to us the hundred and twenty-first psalm.

You'd have thought it was William on the grey horse's back
When (?) chapter he took out his text
As our Orange heroes around him did stand
He explained to us how Stephen been the first Orangeman.

We stood in good order our master to obey,
When the sermon was over we all marched away.
The old gentlemen too as their hats they did raise
Said 'Above all the Lodges, the Cock got the praise.'

Now when returning from Seaforde these Repealers to mind
And the wee Cock Lodge it was coming behind.
Those cowardly rebels, on us they began
They pulled down our wee flag and away they did run.

But our Orange heroes were loyal and true
They soon followed after and made them subdued
and when they overtook them, there on the White Pound
They beat on their hides 'Croppies lie down.'

For whenever we attacked them they put up their Irish cry
'Lord save us from you Cock boys and we'll let you go by,'
And if ever you come to Seaforde and we hope you return
We'll never interfere with your flag, fife or drum.

For all day long those rebels did collect
For as coming home, our wee Lodge to attack
But had they knew we were the boys from the Cock
They'd have took to the mountains and caves of the rocks.

Here's health to young Bleakley wherever he may be
He was worthy of praise, he was our committee
the life of a Thresher he never did dread
With the spear of his pole he cut across a man's head.

Long life to young John McRobert, that hero renown.
He's master of the Lodge that sits in Listooder town
Upon his grey horse which did inspire
For he rode through the heather the Threshers to scare.

Long life to a boy and his name I won't tell
He lives at the Cock and you all know him well
When we were engaged in that bold attack
The house of a Thresher he sent it to wreck.

Now we got home to the Cock all before we did part
And we drunk a full bumper all with our sweethearts
And every glass we took from each other
We said 'Here's to the boy who rode through the heather.'

So God prosper his reverence spoke to us that day
I may finish my song, I have no more to say
And if I'm in the wrong, I hope you'll not me blame
I live in Drumaughlis and you all know my name.[3]

The ballad structure can be a useful device for preserving information, acting as a rhythmic and narrative aide memoir. Among the details recorded here are the fact that the march took place not on July twelfth, but on the thirteenth, the fact that the assembly was addressed by Rev. Boyd, and that several arches were erected in the town of Seaforde in honour of the event. The same event is documented in the *Down Recorder* as follows:

The anniversary of the Battle of the Boyne was celebrated by the Orangemen of this neighbourhood by processions on Monday last, the Twelfth having fallen on a Sunday. Before nine o'clock, some of the lodges began to assemble with drums, colours, and the usual insignia of the order. About half-past ten, twelve lodges belonging to the town and neighbour-hood marched off to Seaforde. The procession was composed of well-dressed individuals, and all was peace and order. They returned in the evening at six o'clock, and soon after separated for their respective homes. The evening, as well as the morning, was characterised by good order, and temperance seemed to have been generally observed. We subjoin an account of the procession at Seaforde from a correspondent:

'The village of Seaforde, on Monday last, presented an animated appearance. Three Orange arches were erected, one on the street which leads to the residence of the Rev. Hugh Smyth Cumming, another opposite the Court-house, and a third at the Boys' School. Several lodges arrived at the village at twelve o'clock, but the great influx commenced about one. The Rev. Charles Boyd, Vicar of Magheradroll, rode at the head of the lodges from Ballynahinch, the Spa, &c. When all had arrived the scene was most magnificent and exhilarating. After the several bodies had refreshed themselves, they proceeded by the Ballynahinch road, and the cut made in the "tenement quarter", to the "point field", in the Rev. W B Forde's demesne, kindly granted for the occasion. There were there assembled fifty-one lodges, containing, with those who accompanied them, upwards of 10,000 persons. The Rev. Mr Boyd addressed the vast multitude from a central eminence, which made a sort of natural platform. After the address, the field resounded with cheers, and the various lodges took the ways leading to their respective homes. The day passed over in peace and quietness. Among those present, were the young gentlemen of the Forde family, and several members of the Rev. Mr Annesley's family.'[4]

All the details listed from the ballad are confirmed, but while the oral account paints a very lively picture, the newspaper stresses 'peace, order . . . and temperance. . .' The same paper records that Orangemen from Castlewellan were also represented that day at Seaforde, adding 'Nine Lodges accompanied them home, as an attack upon them was apprehended, it being the fair day. They reached home in safety.' In addition, it records:

The Benraw and Legananny lodges, belonging to the Rathfriland district, were fired at, on their way home from Rathfriland, on Monday, from two hills, on each side of them. The fire was returned. None of the Orangemen were injured. It is rumoured that two of the assailants are wounded.

Bearing this evidence in mind, it is reasonable to conclude that the ballad provides at least as clear an account of events as does the newspaper. Each account has been composed from a certain standpoint, but the written one has no greater claims to accuracy than the oral.

The oral accounts considered so far are, one way or another, overtly historical in interest. It is perhaps not too difficult to be content that they may, therefore, have historical validity, but what of other types of folklore? Is there any point in arguing over the potential validity of the ghost story or fairy narrative? Consider this example:

It concerns two men . . . two farmers, they lived in Cootehill or Bailieborough, county Cavan and they used to go at the same time every year to the lime kiln for a load of lime you see. It was a long journey to lime kiln and they started off with a horse and cart on the night, about six o'clock in the evening and they wouldn't arrive back from the lime kiln till six in the morning, they'd be all night on the road. Getting their load of lime, on a good night, good moon light night, getting their load of lime and jog back again with it. Well they would arrive about six o'clock in the morning, daylight in the morning, but this particular occasion they sat off as usual in the cart and one of them, not the man that was driving the horse but the other fella put his hand in his pocket to take out his pipe to have a smoke, and when he put his hand in his pocket, took out the pipe and all he found that he had no matches you see. So he told the other man about it he says, 'I went away and forgot my matches,' so that was alright. He says eh, 'When you come,' he says, 'to a house, first light on the road,' he said, 'stop and I'll get a light,' You see? So he said, 'Alright.'

So they drove on and drove on for three or four miles of the road and then they come to this light on the side of the road and he stopped the horse and your man got down off the horse and went down, went in through a gate and down into this house. Now the light of the house was going through the door not the window, through the door, and the window too of course, but he went on into the. . . into the door, he didn't rap he just walked on in as they do in the country you see they don't rap or anything, he just walked on in and there was nobody in the kitchen you see, but there was a big blazing fire on. So he just sat down you know on his hunkers as they call it and he took a piece of the red turf it was a turf fire, piece of the red turf and he put it on the top of his pipe and he pulled the pipe and the pipe lit. And while he was sitting like that in front of the fire he noticed that on the table beside the fire there was two candles burning and then he noticed it that there was a man laid out, a dead man laid out under board. Well now what that meant by underboard was they took the door off and you were laid out on the rail of the table, under the table and the candles and everything that would be attached to the thing, the wake would be lit on the top of the table and in the old days they put the pipe and tobacco and snuff and different things where they you see, that was all on the table, so eh he stood up and he looked at this dead man, and the longer he looked at him the more he knew him, but he couldn't name him, he knew the face so well and he spent I'm sure a good ten minutes gazing at this dead man, nobody else in the kitchen only him.

And the more, and the longer he looked at the man the more he knew him, but yet he couldn't name him. So he had to leave the kitchen and he was still smoking the pipe, he left the kitchen and he came up to the cart and he got up into the cart and the man that was driving the horse never spoke. He says, 'That's a very strange thing that's after happening there,' he says, 'When I went into that house, there was a corp laid out you see on the table underboard,' and says he, 'I couldn't tell who he was, I knew him so well but I couldn't name him.' But the other man who was driving the horse he never spoke, never opened his mouth, so that was forgotten about they drove on to the. . . the lime kiln and they got their load of lime and they came back again and he made no further references to it. And when they came to this spot, where this house was it was just breaking daylight in the morning and he stopped the horse and cart. Now he says, 'Where is your house? Where did you get a light of the pipe?' There was the ruins of the house, just the four walls of the house where he had got the light of the pipe, there was no house there and there hadn't been for a generation or two before it. So there you are that was the end of the story.[5]

This story is a sophisticated development of a very well known basic theme, that of experiences in a house later discovered to be in ruins, an oral exploration of the possibility of time travel and dimensional confusion. In this example, it is essential to the narrative that the central character is not immediately aware of the ghost. This is achieved by the apparently unlikely device of hiding the corpse under the wake table. The irony is that this apparently unlikely narrative twist is actually a device whereby a piece of historical information is preserved. Henry Morris explains how,

> . . . when the corpse was washed and dressed for the coffin, it was placed under the table, not on the floor but on a shelf about eight or nine inches off the floor . . . old tables had two rails fixed longitudinally about this height from the floor and a door-leaf or some boards made an improvised shelf on which the corpse was laid out. In South Ulster as well as in North Connacht, the corpse was always laid out in this fashion, under the table; in Co. Donegal, on the other hand, the corpse was placed on the table.[6]

In some parts of South Armagh, the word 'underboard' can still occasionally be heard in reference to a dead person. In seventeenth-century Ireland, the practice must have been much more widespread, for during his time as bishop of Waterford early in the 1680s, John Brennan remarked 'It is the custom in this country at the Requiem to place the corpse under the table. . .'.[7] In this way, factual material may be embedded and preserved in sources which may appear unpromising.

In addition to contributing in these ways to knowledge of the past, folklore may help to inform the cultural climate of the past. The following story at first may appear to be little more than a fanciful narrative confection, but is worth closer analysis:

> Years ago, maybe even today, they used to believe in the fairies and used to see them quite a lot. In fact there's some ones'll tell you even yet that they've seen them. But this was a very stormy, a very stormy night you see, blowing a gale, and rain, sleet, and there was a woman lived at the far end of the island. She was a nurse-cum-midwife. She done everything, you see.
>
> So, she was in bed this night and a knock came to the door, and I said it was a very, very stormy night, and she went to the door, and there was – at that time there was no such thing as a four-wheeled coach on the island. The only ones had a carriage was the Gages – and she went to the door and this team of four horses and a four-wheeled coach was outside the door, and there was a man with it, and she thought it very strange. At first she thought she was dreaming, but then she knew, she realized there was something strange about it and the man, she couldn't see him in the darkness. He said that she was needed, there was a woman in labour and they needed her very urgently, and, so she knew, and decided that no harm would come to her, that she'd get into the coach.
>
> So, she got into the coach, and it set off down the road, and if I was at the far end of the island I could point out the place to you. Set off across bogs, round the side of the hill where there was no road, and across a bog you know, a very marshy place. It didn't sink in the bog. And they arrived at this hill at the back of Brockley. And as they come to the hill, the side of the hill opened up and the horse and carriage went into the hill. And inside it, you know it was the most beautiful place, it was like a palace inside it. There was everything you could imagine in it. And before this there was a lot of islanders going missing, and young girls, and young men in the island going missing. And nobody ever knew what was happening, they thought that they were maybe being kidnapped, you know somebody coming to the island by boat and taking them off it. It was put down to this.
>
> But anyway inside the hill; there was a palace inside the hill, the woman recognized a lot of them. And anyway she attended to the woman that was giving birth and everything was sorted out. But I forgot to add here, that there was a lot of fairies running around, the wee folk, there was a lot of them in this hill you see. And they went to her and they said to her that they would give her anything to stay. So, 'No', she said. 'No.' She wouldn't. And then they offered her something to eat and she was going to, she was quite hungry, so she decided it wouldn't do any harm, she would take something to eat. But just by the side of the fire there was a young girl sitting nursing a small baby and she was singing to it in Gaelic. Now unfortunately I don't

know, don't remember the words in Gaelic, what she was singing, but in English what she was singing to the baby was, 'eat nothing, drink nothing, or don't stay the night.' She was repeating this over and over again in Gaelic. So, this was a warning, you see, to the nurse. So she insisted that they take her back home. So she got into the carriage again, and they left her back to her own door. So she was very upset about all this and, she didn't know what to do about it, so she went down to the landlord, the Gages. She went down to him and she told him about this, and he warned her on peril of her life she was never to mention this to anybody or he would banish her off the island. So she must have mentioned it or the story wouldn't have got out. So that was that. I always thought that was a very nice tale. I used to like to listen to that a lot.[8]

This fairy narrative offers us several insights into a cultural climate which by virtue of the material with which it deals, has become unfamiliar. It can be considered from a general perspective and from a viewpoint more specifically localised. The story type is a widespread and familiar one, but this specific version has been tailored to Rathlin. We are made aware of this quite early on, through the comment, 'The only ones had a carriage was the Gages . . .', this being the landlord's family on the island. The Gages regularly appear in Rathlin folklore, sometimes as the primary focus of a tale, very often in an incidental reference such as this. These references illustrate the closely interwoven nature of Rathlin society and the fact that the landlord and his family were constantly present in the consciousness of the islanders. The tale also makes detailed reference to the Rathlin landscape, and in part this helps to localise and actualise the supernatural aspects of the story. The main action of the narrative occurs at a place called Brockley. This is very significant, as Brockley is a well known archaeological site. Fairy narrative frequently features archaeological landmarks. As a generality, ancient earthworks are often referred to as fairy forts, and specific sites may in a story become a fairy habitation or as in this case, provide an appropriate locale for the supernatural. As W. B. Yeats enquires:

> Is the fairy-kingdom the world of the past, continuing in its own place, and divided by only a thin veil of time from our own? The traditional respect for 'forts', raths, fairy-trees and other fairy-haunts, which farmer and hedger will not disturb, is perhaps a respect (as for the treasures in a tomb) due to what belongs, in some measure, still to its former owners. In usurping the earth which others tilled and loved, and above all their holy places, does it not behove the living to tread softly? Has not our urban and profane civilisation, in obliterating old landmarks, become impoverished as by a loss of memory?[9]

It is by means of issues such as this that folklore informs and thus may bring the local historian into closer contact with the 'cultural climate' of the past. Fairy lore illuminates a network of beliefs in which the natural is constantly penetrated by the supernatural, so that the supernatural may as a matter of course directly influence natural experience. In the story cited, this is in relation to childbirth, but music, dairying, death and other matters are equally likely to be treated in this way. A closer look at the Rathlin tale reveals that it too deals with death as well as with birth. The young woman whose warning alerts the midwife not to eat or drink in order to avoid partaking of fairy nature, is a representative of the droves of people said by folklore to have been the subject of fairy abduction. Babies, brides, musicians and women in childbirth were among those believed to be at greatest risk. In this way, the fairy world may be said to overlap with the world of the dead, more commonly thought of as the preserve of ghost lore. The Rathlin midwife tale is an excellent example of a specialised, local, orally transmitted variant of a widely known plot type, providing clear illustrations of both the localisation of an oral narrative and of its more general applicability. Both aspects are of relevance to the local historian.

There is another dimension to this issue. To a large extent, a specific oral variant of a narrative is shaped by the narrator, but it can be demonstrated that variants also display aspects of regionalisation. A Galway version of a tale (for instance) may differ in certain readily definable ways from a variant of the same story told (for example) in Antrim. The process by which this happens is known as 'oicotypification', and the local historian may justifiably be concerned with discovering if any such patterning may be discerned in the folklore of a given region.[10]

Folklore may be concerned with matters other than the study of narrative and of oral history. It may provide information about local speech patterns, dialect and language. It offers the opportunity to consider matters as diverse as proverbs and cures. Local poetry is often orally preserved, and we have already had evidence of the potential value of ballad and song.

Particularly in Ireland, studies of folklore often concern themselves with material of the types illustrated by the examples chosen above. While these help to establish the potential value of folklore as a source for the local historian, there is another dimension, also of great potential importance, one which is all too often neglected to such a degree that its actual existence has in fact been questioned. Some forty years ago, A. T. Lucas commented upon 'the almost total absence [in Ireland] of anything in the nature of folk art', and went on to cite the example of needlework to help illustrate his point, making the rather extraordinary claim that 'textiles are severely plain, needlework is strictly utilitarian'.[11] The local historian whose concern is with an area of linen production may immediately find this claim surprising, and it has broader implications for a vast wealth of material of relevance to the study of both folk and decorative art. Items of this type have also suffered neglect in England, causing Peter Brears to remark,

> It is extremely difficult for anyone to gain access to collections of English folk art, to such an extent that its very existence has come to be in doubt.[12]

The local historian becoming concerned with folklore as a source of information may well wish to address issues raised by material culture, an area so far relatively unexploited by researchers.

Available sources for the study of material of this kind fall into three broad types. There are those available in published form, for example in the Ordnance Survey Memoirs and in other publications, particularly in nineteenth- and early twentieth-century descriptions of life in Ireland as a whole or in specific regions.[13] There are archival resources such as those preserved at the Department of Folklore in University College, Dublin, and at the Ulster Folk and Transport Museum. In recent years there has been activity in other areas, for example under the auspices of University College, Cork. The final and perhaps the most important resource is fieldwork. The local historian may unearth rich sources of information by interviewing and recording material actually available orally in the geographical area to be researched. After transcription, such material may usefully be analysed, and may also make an important contribution to an existing archive in which it may be of further value to subsequent students and researchers.[14]

Folklore may provide the historian with direct accounts of important past events. It may supply rich evidence of often hitherto uninvestigated aspects of local social history. It may illuminate the past by providing evidence of systems of popular belief by means of which experience was ordered and understood. It has the capacity to extend and enrich the scope of historical knowledge, and is among the useful and powerful sources available to the researcher.

1. Ulster Folk and Transport Museum Reel Recording [hereafter UFTM R] 81.16.
2. UFTM R 83.151. For a study of this and related oral material see L. M. Ballard, 'Just whatever they had handy. . . ' in *Ulster Folklife* xxxi (1985).
3. UFTM C.78.109.
4. *Down Recorder*, 18 July 1846.
5. UFTM C.76.50.

6. Henry Morris, 'Irish wake games' in *Bealoideas* viii (1938), pp. 127 and 128.

7. Rev. P. Canon Power (ed.), *A bishop of the penal times* (Cork, 1932), p. 32. I am indebted to Raymond Gillespie for this reference.

8. UFTM C.79.29.

9. W. B. Yeats (ed.), *Fairy and folk tales of Ireland* (Gerrard's Cross, 1973), p. ix. Earthworks are also often referred to as 'Danes' forts', an issue the implications of which are addressed by L. M. Smith in 'The Position of the 'Danes' in contemporary Ulster oral narrative' in *Ulster Folklife* xxv (1979).

10. For a case study, see L. M. Ballard, 'The formulation of the oicotype' in *Fabula* xxiv (1983). See also C. W. von Sydow, 'Geography and folktale oicotypes', in *Selected papers on folklore* (Copenhagen, 1948).

11. A. T. Lucas, 'Folklife' in *A view of Ireland* (Dublin, 1957), p. 204.

12. Peter Brears, *North country folk art* (Edinburgh, 1989), p. 3.

13. For example, the early to mid nineteenth-century accounts by Rev. Caesar Otway are valuable sources of relevant material.

14. Occasional seminars on fieldwork and recording techniques are held at the Ulster Folk and Transport Museum.

READING THE PAST:
LITERATURE AND LOCAL HISTORY

Myrtle Hill

In 1985, the editorial team of a journal entitled *Literature and History*, committed to an interdisciplinary approach to the past, responded to the query,

> Why should we interest ourselves seriously in the once–upon–a–time
> worlds of fiction – these unreal stories about unreal individuals?

with the admission that it is 'a question more easily asked than answered'.[1]
The intention of this essay is to address this task, more with the hope of stimulating interest and suggesting guidelines, than of providing a definitive solution to the problems involved. For the relationship between literature and local history is both fascinating and complex. Although the 'telling of stories' is central to each discipline, there the similarities would seem to end. One type of 'story' is perceived to be a 'real' account – apparently true, factual, the result of scientific enquiry – while the other is regarded as a subjective work of creative imagination. Any interaction between the two subject areas would thus seem to be fraught with contradictions.

However, while we should not underestimate the difficulties, the distinctions between the two disciplines are by no means so clear-cut as they at first appear. 'History' is more than an objective accumulation of facts, it is a narrative upon which meaning is constructed by the narrator/historian, and while the discipline sets limits to an individual's interpretation in terms of accuracy and evidence, there are invariably not one, but several histories of any one event or period. Each version is the result of careful research and analysis, and one no less valid than the other – they are simply stories told from different perspectives – the long-running 'revisionist' debate in Irish historiography provides a graphic example of the multiple possibilities.

During the course of the twentieth century, women's history, labour history and the histories of minority groups have introduced new dimensions into the traditional historical accounts of the victorious and the powerful. This concern to uncover the experience of marginalised groups in society has resulted in the more imaginative use of a wider range of source materials. Oral history, photographs, folklore and mythology have all been deployed to aid in the reconstruction of the lives of those traditionally 'hidden from history'. Works of literature have of course had their place in these developments, and while accessing the past through this particular route brings its own methodological problems, the process can be enjoyable and the rewards significant.

I

In the most basic sense, poems and novels are of value for their descriptive passages, providing evidence of places, occupations or manners. We can learn much about the fashionable lifestyle of the English gentry, for example, from the novels of Jane Austen. Sensitively and carefully approached, imaginative literature can light up a period in a way which more traditional historical evidence can not; it can humanise statistics and make the study of the past more interesting. This is perhaps particularly true of the nineteenth century, when the concern of novelists with the social changes of the world they inhabited was reflected in their fictional works: as a contemporary reviewer put it in 1850, 'books of fictions are all now connected in some way with the condition of society'.[2] The novels of Mrs Elizabeth Gaskell, for example, particularly *Mary Barton* and *North and South*, are fine examples of this genre, telling us more of the experience of working-class life in early nineteenth-century Manchester than a roomful of 'Blue Books'. While Gaskell herself made use of the wealth of statistical detail compiled by civil servants, her fictional work suggests a more complex approach to economic categorisation. In *Mary Barton: A Tale of Manchester Life* (2 volumes, 1848) the reader is made aware of the different levels of poverty subsumed within the term 'working class'. The trajectory ranges from the destitution of out-of-work cellar-dwellers, through the bleak existence of those in marginal employment, to the relative comforts of homes where at least one family member is earning a regular wage. The developing storyline also reveals the precarious nature of life for the poor at all levels and demonstrates how incidents such as a strike, illness or death, or a fire at the mill, can dramatically change the standards of family life.

Mrs Gaskell's acute observation, close knowledge of Manchester working-class life and literary imagination combine to produce a complex, multi-layered and 'realistic' portrait of everyday life. That on occasion her concern with social issues was to the detriment of the novel's plot, is an unfortunate consequence, much regretted by literary critics. For the social historian, however, the novel's 'flaws', particularly the overly-intrusive authorial comments, are themselves an intricate element of the source material. Mrs Gaskell's proclaimed intention in *Mary Barton* was not merely to chronicle the living and working conditions of the Manchester poor, but to bring the realities of their life to the attention of those with the power to make a difference. Like many of her literary contemporaries, this wife of a Unitarian minister believed that the dispelling of mutual ignorance would bridge the widening gap between the 'Two Nations' identified in Benjamin Disraeli's earlier flight of literary fancy,[3] and thus encourage a more humane and harmonious approach to social problems. Moreover, contemporary responses suggest that the novel was received in just such a spirit:

> People on Turkey carpets, with their three meat meals a day, are wondering, forsooth, why working men turn Chartists and Communists. Do they want to know why? Then let them read *Mary Barton*. Do they want to know why poor men, kind and sympathising as women to each other, learn to hate law and order, Queen, Lords and Commons, country-party and corn-law leagues, all alike, to hate the rich in short? Then let them read *Mary Barton*.[4]

The 1990s reader of the novel, however, not only gains insight into the world of Manchester millworkers, trade unionists and employers, but, through the didactic tone, with its social and moral purpose clearly outlined, and the middle-class values of its author determining much of the action, can tap into the hopes and fears, perceptions and anxieties which preoccupied the writer and her generation. *Mary Barton* is only one of a group of novels written in the 1840s which, since the mid-twentieth century have been acknowledged as a valid means of accessing the 'frame of mind' of a generation struggling with the practical and moral problems generated by the new industrial age.[5]

II

But let us, like the local historian, be more geographically specific. In his 1938 poem, *Epic*, Patrick Kavanagh celebrated the local perspective:

> I have lived in important places, times
> When great events were decided, who owned
> That half a rood of rock, a no-man's land
> Surrounded by our pitchforked-armed claims.
> I heard the Duffys shouting 'Damn your Soul'
> And old McCabe stripped to the waist, seen
> Step the plot defying blue cast-steel –

'Here is the march along these iron stones'
That was the year of the Munich bother. Which
Was more important? I inclined
To lose my faith in Ballyrush and Gortin
Till Homer's ghost came whispering to my mind
He said: I made the Iliad from such
A local row. Gods make their own importance.[6]

Kavanagh's 'triumphant reversal'[7] is more than an attempt to justify the poet's focus on his county Monaghan home. The reference to Homer's *Iliad*, suggesting a relationship between the 'local row' and the 'Munich bother', points to the universality of human experience – the transcending of time and place – which is for many both the purpose and defining characteristic of great art. Perhaps contrary to expectations, however, the local historian will usually find the work of minor poets and novelists more rewarding and revealing than that of the major talents. To study a piece of literature as an historical document requires the employment of different criteria from those used by the literary critic; while universality is applauded by the latter, a strong sense of time and place and a grounding in specific details is of much greater value to the former. As we have noted earlier, it follows too that distinctions between 'good' and 'bad' literature undergo some kind of revision in the hands of the historical explorer.

In a study of James Orr, the late eighteenth-century 'Bard of Ballycarry', Don Akenson and Bill Crawford demonstrate how the work of a minor poet, while perhaps not of great literary merit, can add a 'qualitative third-dimensional aspect' to contemporary documents.[8] As their analysis clearly demonstrates, the relation between the late eighteenth-century Ulster poet and his local community was unique: financially supported by those whose views he was called upon to represent, such an artist produced for his neighbours, not abstract, philosophic or private contemplations, but poems 'about such things as earning a living, food, social customs, local topography, notable personages, and, of course, death, tragic and not so tragic'.[9] While Orr was himself a remarkable individual – 'a rebel, an emigrant, and a convivial raconteur'[10] – he shared the values and experiences of many of his neighbours, and his writings are thus a fascinating source for the local historian with an interest in politics (particularly pertinent in this instance are the changing local views on national and international events), religion, emigration and a wide range of social customs, habits and superstitions.

A point made by the authors of this study, and much more generally applicable, is the importance of contextualising both the poetry and the poet. No documentary source can of course be studied in isolation, but when the primary evidence is a poem or novel the need for validation is even more significant. In this invaluable little publication Akenson and Crawford include a collection of more traditional documentary materials which provide a range of alternative perspectives on the issues dealt with by the poet. While the historian does not need to become a literary critic, nor the student of literature an expert in the past, there is no doubt that the labours of each can be substantially enriched by such cross-fertilisation.

III

We have briefly considered the nineteenth-century English novel, but novels of value to the local historian can also be found on this side of the Irish Sea. Indeed, it is a young woman from county Longford who is credited with writing the 'first regional novel'. The recent reprinting of Maria Edgeworth's *Castle Rackrent* in the World's Classics[11] series is fitting recognition of the importance of this work, both in its own right and in the wider literary tradition. Also acclaimed as 'the first socio-historical novel, the first Irish novel, the first Big House novel, the first saga novel',[12] this groundbreaking work was enormously popular amongst early nineteenth-century readers, and was to be a major influence on later writers. Quite apart from its value as a 'good read' in its own right, this story of several generations of landlords in county Longford offers today's readers valuable insights into landlord-tenant relations in pre-Famine Ireland. Published on the eve of the Union between Britain and Ireland, the narrative points up the complexities in Irish social life all too often lost in current revisionist debates, and introduces the reader to a memorable range of comic characters, vividly brought to life by a young Anglo-Irish woman of considerable wit and ability.

When Richard Edgeworth arrived in Ireland in 1782, his eldest daughter, then aged fifteen, closely involved herself in all the legal, financial and other day-to-day business of managing his 600-acre estate. By her father's side as he sought to modernise and introduce more humane practices into a system of landlordism hampered by generations of irresponsibility, ignorance, and exploitation, Maria had a unique opportunity to observe the language, custom and habits of the ordinary Irish men and women with whom she was to people her first and most famous novel. Indeed in an oft-quoted letter, Richard Lovell Edgeworth referred with considerable pride to the use to which her work had been put:

> We hear from very good authority that the king was much pleased with Castle Rackrent – he rubbed his hands and said, 'What, what – I know something now of my Irish subjects'.[13]

Although she had already collaborated with her father on several educational publications, Maria's authorial experiments in *Castle Rackrent* were to have an important impact on the embryonic novel form. The satirical account of the decline of the Rackrent family is ostensibly told by Thady Quirk, an old family retainer who asserts his devoted loyalty to each of his new masters in turn: the excessively hospitable Sir Patrick, the litigious and oppressive Sir Murtagh, neglectful absentee Sir Kit and finally the unfortunate, indebted Sir Condy who sells the property to Thady's son, Jason. Thus the fall of the Rackrents, once descended from kings of Ireland, is paralleled by the rise of the native Irish dispossessed. Perhaps most potently symbolic in this process is the failure of the irresponsible, weak family line to reproduce itself. Interestingly, in a world where relationships are characterised by cruelty and selfishness, the Rackrent women somehow always manage to survive and out-wit their partners. The ironic depiction of the uses and abuses of power is enriched by the complex nature of Thady's narrative, for, despite his con-stant assurances of loyalty to the Big House, in his dialogue with the reader he becomes a three-dimensional participant in events. Such sophisticated lit-erary devices actually reinforce rather than invalidate the novel's historical interest as the condemnations, the comedy and the silences of his story reflect a range of perspectives on the source and consequences of misrule. Consider, for example, Thady's description of Lady Murtagh:

> my lady was very charitable in her own way. She had a charity school for poor children, where they were taught to read and write gratis, and where they were kept well to spinning gratis for my lady in return; for she always had heaps of duty yarn from the tenants, and got all her household linen out of the estate from first to last; for after the spining, the weavers on the estate took it in hand for nothing, because of the looms my lady's interests could get from the Linen Board to distribute gratis. Then there was a bleach yard near us, and the tenant dare refuse my lady nothing, for fear of a law-suit Mr. Murtagh kept hanging over him about the water course. With these ways of managing, 'tis surprising how cheap my lady got things done, and how proud she was of it. Her table the same way – kept for next to nothing – duty fowls, and duty turkies, and duty geese, came as fast as we could eat 'em, for my lady kept a sharp look out, and knew to a tub of butter every thing the tenants had, all round. They knew her way, and what with fear of driving for rent and Sir Murtagh's lawsuits, they were kept in such good order, they never thought of coming near Castle Stopgap with a present of something of other – nothing too much or too little for my lady – eggs – honey – butter – meal – fish – game – grouse, and herrings, fresh or salt – all went for something. As for their young pigs, we had them, and the best bacon and hams they could make up, with all young chickens in spring, but they were a set of poor wretches.[14]

Edgeworth set her story in 1782, claiming in the preface that her portrayal represented an older generation of Anglo-Irish landlords, and she looked to the Union between Britain and Ireland with a degree of optimism. In a letter to her brother in 1834, however, she confessed her disillusionment, stating that to depict the current Irish scene was beyond her power:

> It is impossible to draw Ireland as she now is in the book of fiction – realities are too strong, party passions too violent, to bear to see, or care to look at their faces in a looking glass. The people would only break the glass and curse the fool who held the mirror up to nature – distorted nature in a fever.[15]

In the complex and contentious area of Anglo-Irish relations, *Castle Rackrent* remains as a testimony to Edgeworth's insight, humour and literary talent, as well as an enjoyable and thought-provoking read.

The work of William Carleton (1794–1869) has also been acknowledged as an important source for the social historian. As the youngest (fourteenth) son of a tenant farmer from county Tyrone, Carleton's hedge-school education and carefree youth provided him with abundant materials for the lively tales of Irish peasant life which have themselves become an important part of our cultural heritage. Close familiarity with and direct experience of his subject matter gave life and vigour to Carleton's portrayals of local events and characters, ensuring their popularity with more than one generation of delighted readers. *Traits and Stories of the Irish Peasantry*, first published in 1830, went through several editions, and was followed by a second series in 1833. A twentieth-century novelist described the impact of Carleton's writing:

> William Carleton of Prillisk in the County Tyrone steps out from the pages of his own tales. He is Jemmy McEvoy, the Poor Scholar traveling hopefully towards Maynooth, he is Denis O'Shaughnessy hurrying homeward from Maynooth to wed 'the cream of his affections', Susy Connor, he is Shane Fadh, who before the eyes of his sweetheart, could out-dance, out-throw, out-speed all his rivals in the glades of Althadhawan Wood.[16]

It is of course the general scarcity of documentary evidence on pre-Famine peasant life which renders these stories so valuable to the historian of the period, and of course they also deal with aspects of popular culture difficult to find in the more traditional historical archive. Wakes and weddings, faction fights, country dances, drinking dens and sporting rivalries – events at the very core of community life – are vividly recorded.

However, like Elizabeth Gaskell and Maria Edgeworth, Carleton too was self-consciously writing for a purpose, placing himself in the role of historical chronicler:

I found them a class unknown in literature, unknown by their landlords, and unknown by those in whose hands much of their destiny was placed. If I became the historian of their habits and manners, their feelings, their prejudices, their superstitions, and their crimes, if I have attempted to delineate their moral, religious and physical state, it was because I saw no person willing to undertake a task which surely must be looked upon as an important one. I was anxious that those who ought, but did not understand their character, should know them, not merely for selfish purposes, but that they should teach them to know themselves and appreciate their rights, both moral and civil, as rational men, who owe obedience to law, without the necessity of being a slave either to priest or landlord.[17]

Carleton's anxiety on this point undoubtedly affected the tone and quality of his writing, and, in the view of many critics, considerably detracted from their enjoyment of the story. As one mid nineteenth-century reviewer put it,

one of the merits of Mr. Carleton's best tales is, that they convey their own lessons, and require no gloss. When he epitomises himself into a lecture, it is like the exquisite singing of a beautiful song followed by a drawling recitation of the words.'[18]

Narrative intrusion was of course a well-known literary device of the period, by no means unique to Carleton, but fact and fantasy often sat uneasily together. Carleton's *The Black Prophet* is a case in point. Written during the tragic 1840s, Carleton set this 'ripping yarn' amidst the devastation of an earlier period of famine, making plain in the dedication to the prime minister, Lord John Russell, that there was an underlying serious message about economic realities and the British government's responsibilities in Ireland.[19] As a melodramatic murder story, it has been judged inconsistent and unconvincing, however, its dark mood and sombre atmosphere powerfully evoke the tenor of the times in which he wrote:

the incessant rain accompanied by warmth which produced rotting crops; the horror of the famine fever; the makeshift lean-to sheds for the sick and dying by the roadside; the shallow graves which scarcely concealed the diseased corpses; the starving peasants grubbing for nettles and watercress by road and brook; the riots and attacks on provision carts heading for the ports with precious food intended for export.[20]

While there is little agreement among literary critics about Carleton's place in Irish literary tradition, the value of his writings in providing an insight into the world of pre-Famine Ireland is not contested.[21] The didactic stance which proved so controversial in literary terms does not pose the same problems for historians – so long as we are aware of that stance. Indeed, in the case of *The Black Prophet*, critic John Cronin argues that it is only when the author moves from fact to fiction that problems occur – arguing that Carleton is better at portraying the reality around him, than dealing with the more fantastic elements of the tale.[22]

The importance of recognising and acknowledging the writer's agenda is of course not only applicable to literary works, but to all documentary sources – all 'evidence' is written from a particular perspective, for a specific purpose and readership. The local historian needs to acquaint him or herself with the motivation and personality of the author, to be aware of what she/he is trying to express through their work. We need to know where their sympathies lie, and to take account of any bias in our interpretation of their writings.

Other factors which need to be taken into consideration when assessing the value of fictional material to the historian suggest the more serious and subtle limitations of the exercise. A 'realistic' or true-to-life approach can be considerably constrained by the mechanics of novel-writing; for example, an author may well be obliged to deviate from the probable to the fairly implausible in the interests of character development or in order to meet the requirements of the plot – the more sensational or melodramatic elements of a story might simply be accounted for by the demands of serialisation – nail-biting, cliffhanging situations at the end of a section would ensure a captive audience for the next instalment. The need to 'tie up' the various threads of a story-line on the novel's completion frequently led to 'unrealistic' happy endings with marriage usually symbolising harmony and resolution – a far cry from the psychological realism of the late twentieth century! We need to be clear that it is not usually the story-line itself which is of most value to the historical researcher, but the backdrop, where sensitivity to setting, character and social nuance can be acutely revealing.

Anthony Trollope is perhaps best known for his series of Barchester stories, but in his very first published novel this popular nineteenth-century writer focused on the plight of the Irish poor and on conditions witnessed at first hand during the first six years of his sojourn on the island. *The MacDermots of Ballycloran*, first published in 1847, has been largely overlooked by scholars of literature. But while its literary merit may be debatable, it is generally agreed that Trollope's story, which he finished writing only months before the first appearance of the potato blight, contains much of value in its depiction of life in rural Ireland on the eve of the Great Famine. Set in county Leitrim in the 1830s, the story revolves around the misfortunes of a family of the old Irish Catholic gentry class, describing the decline of an already marginalised landlord. Through the plot the reader is introduced to drinking dens, a wedding party, a race meeting, secret societies and local legal proceedings. We are given a strong sense of the different levels of poverty in the locality, of the problems of debt, mortgages, rent collection and the constant threat of eviction. In this tale of seduction and murder, the vitality and energy as well as the tensions within and between the various classes and professions in Irish society are graphically, though often comically, described. The following extract is a fine example of Trollope's style in this early novel:

> We must now request our reader to accompany us to the little town of Mohill; not that there is anything attractive in the place to repay him for the trouble of going there. Mohill is a small country town, standing on no high road, nor on any thoroughfare from the metropolis; and therefore it owes to itself whatever importance it may possess – and, in truth, that is not much. It is, or at any rate, was, at the time of which we are writing, the picture of an impoverished town – the property of a non-resident landlord – destitute of anything to give it interest or prosperity – without business, without trade, and without society. The idea that would strike one on entering it was chiefly this: 'Why was it a town at all? – why were there, on that spot, so many houses congregated, called Mohill? – what was the inducement to people to come and live there? – Why didn't they go to Longford, to Cavan, to Carrick, to Dublin, – anywhere rather than there, when they were going to settle themselves?' This is a question which proposes itself at the sight of so many Irish towns; they look so poor, so destitute of advantage, so unfriended. Mohill is by no means the only town in the west of Ireland, that strikes one as being there without a cause.
>
> It is built on the side of a steep hill, and one part of the town seems constantly threatening the destruction of the other. Every now and again, down each side of the hill, there is a slated house, but they are few and far between; and the long spaces intervening are filled with the most miserable descriptions of cabins – hovels without chimneys, windows, door, or signs of humanity, except the children playing on the collected filth in front of them. The very scraughs of which the roofs are composed are germinating afresh, and, sickly green with a new growth, look more like the tops of long-neglected dungheaps, than the only protection over Christian beings from the winds of heaven.
>
> Look at that hovel on the left, which seems as if it had thrust itself between its neighbours, so narrow is its front! The roof, looking as if it were only the dirty eaves hanging from its more aspiring neighbour on the right, supports itself against the cabin on the left, about three feet above the ground. Can that be the habitation of any of the human race? Few but such as those whose lot has fallen on such barren places would venture in; but for a moment let us see what is there.

But the dark misery within hides itself in thick obscurity. The unaccus-
tomed eye is at first unable to distinguish any object, and only feels the
painful effect of the confined smoke; but when, at length, a faint struggling
light makes its way through the entrance, how wretched is all around!

A sickly woman, the entangled nature of whose insufficient garments
would defy description, is sitting on a low stool before the fire, suckling a
miserably dirty infant; a boy, whose only covering is a tattered shirt, is
putting fresh, but alas, damp turf beneath the pot in which are put to boil
the potatoes – their only food. Two or three dim children – their number is
lost in their obscurity – are cowering round the dull, dark fire, atop of one
another; and on a miserable pallet beyond – a few rotten boards, propped
upon equally infirm supports, and covered over with only one thin black
quilt – is sitting the master of the mansion; his grizzly, unshorn beard, his
lantern jaws and shaggy hair, are such as his home and family would lead
one to expect. And now you have counted all that this man possesses; other
furniture has he none – neither table nor chair, except that low stool on
which his wife is sitting. Squatting on the ground – from off the ground,
like pigs, only much more poorly fed – his children eat the scanty earnings
of his continual labour. And yet for this abode the man pays rent.[23]

In this passage we can really appreciate the power of literary talent applied to
the act of description. As we wander down the track into the village of
Mohill, with our companionable author and guide, we not only see through
his eyes, but collude with his judgement. The 'thrusting hovel', with its roof
supporting itself against its neighbour, and the germinating sickly green of
the roof, are suggestive of the human weakness, disease, suffering and disintegration which are Trollope's major concern. The poverty of its inhabitants
graphically and immediately strikes our senses as we peer into the smoky
dark interior amongst the cowering children, whose numbers are lost in
murky obscurity. This is a harsh piece of social criticism in which the literary devices add to rather than detract from the overall realism of the scene.
The pointed criticism of the damning final sentence requires no further
comment. Trollope's own assessment of his first novel, is I think fair:

The *Macdermots* is a good novel, and worth reading by anyone who wishes
to understand what Irish life was before the potato disease, the famine, and
the Encumbered Estates Bill.[24]

To properly evaluate Trollope's description, the local historian can draw on
a range of more traditional materials on nineteenth-century country towns;
the Ordnance Survey Memoirs, many of which have now been published, are
particularly valuable in this exercise. Contemporary biographies and autobi-

ographies are also useful 'alternative' sources, as are the many accounts written by those who visited Ireland to assess and report on conditions there.[25]

The Kellys and the O'Kellys (1848) and *Castle Richmond* (1860) were also set in Ireland, but it was in his last novel, left unfinished after his death following a stroke in 1882, that Trollope was again to address the profound difficulties of that country. By this stage Irish political life was dominated at both the popular and official level by the land question, and the main plot of *The Landleaguers* focuses closely on the contemporary struggle between landlords and tenants. The action takes place in county Galway, and revolves around the tensions between the English-born landlord, Philip Jones, local tenant farmers, and the physical force element in rural politics. The novel, in part a detailed documentary record of events in both Westminster and the Irish countryside, demonstrates the complexity of social relationships, with divided loyalties and personal antagonisms as well as political ideology providing the motivation for acts of boycott and murder. Thus, when Jones goes to court seeking retribution for the actions of the Land League, following the murder of his son,

> it may be imagined that the trial was not commenced in Galway without the expression of much sympathy for Mr. Jones and the family at Morony Castle. It is hard to explain the different feelings which existed, feelings exactly opposed to each other, but which still were both in their way general and true. He was 'poor Mr. Jones', who had lost his son, and worse still, his eighty acres of grass, and he was also 'that fellow Jones, that enemy to the Landleague, whom it behoved all patriotic Irishmen to get the better of and to conquer.[26]

Trollope's novel is considerably enriched, for both the general reader and the social historian, by a sub-plot dealing with the contemporary debate on women's rights, both in employment and in society more generally. *The Landleaguers*, which did not enjoy popular success, nonetheless provided Trollope with a 'distinct means of representing the disintegration of social bonds, community life, and political coherence that were underway at the moment of writing'.[27]

Reflecting the social and political significance of their subject matter, novels focusing on the 'Big House' have played a particularly important role in the Irish literary tradition. From Edgeworth's *Castle Rackrent* (1800) to Jennifer Johnston's *The Captains and the Kings* (1972), 'Big House' novels have described and commented upon the decline of a class and a way of life which affected entire communities. The strains and tensions between the worlds of privilege and want, at a time when relations between the two were undergoing political, social and economic change, provided authors such as George Moore, Somerville and Ross and Elizabeth Bowen with a dynamic backdrop for their powerful stories. The symbolic setting and the different nuances of speech, customs and ways of behaviour which separate the classes, combined with atmospheric description, resulted in a genre which has developed its own historiography and which is invaluable to those seeking local colour, whether in the late nineteenth or early twentieth century. As one critic put it:

> Today little remains of these great houses, but a great deal of the society and culture which peopled the big house is alive in Irish literature. . . Arranged chronologically, Big House fiction is a reflection of, as well as a reflection on, economic, social and political change. Accordingly, as a point where fact and fiction meet, it has attracted both the literary critic and the historian. . .[28]

From the second half of the nineteenth century, the massive popularity of the novel form resulted in a wealth of literature which can help to throw light on a wide range of social, economic and political issues. The constant reprinting of many of the classics is evidence of their enduring quality and their popularity amongst readers of all ages. However, the recent reprinting of several minor works suggests that their value in more than literary terms is now being recognised. Read with the aid of a thoughtful, historically-based introduction, these fictional tales can be an important addition to the archives of the local historian, whether amateur or professional.

IV

We have already noted that William Carleton was an important early exponent of the short-story form, and in our own century writers such as James Joyce, Frank O'Connor and Daniel Corkery made use of this genre to introduce new insights into both urban and rural life. Whether our interests lie in the shabby gentility of lower-middle-class Dublin, the struggle of man to make a living out of the land in counties Cork and Kerry, or with the psychological effects of political turmoil, our quest for knowledge – and understanding – can be significantly enhanced by such narratives. A host of minor writers have also left fictional accounts of life in early twentieth-century Ireland to both amuse and educate the reader. I shall mention only a few which I have found useful in my work on the north-east: Shan Bullock's portrayal of Protestant communities around Lough Erne, in novels such as *The Squireen* (1903) and *The Loughsiders* (1924); St John Ervine's realistic Belfast novels of the interwar years; *The Bush that Burned* (1931) in which Lydia Foster brings to life the ethos of late nineteenth-century Ulster

Presbyterianism, dominated by the ageing Henry Cooke and revivalist Tommy Toye.

More enduring in terms of literary strength was Sam Hanna Bell's perceptive tale of love and tragedy set on the shores of Strangford Lough at the turn of the century. *December Bride* (1951) traces change and continuity, the role of religion and the place of women in a tight-knit community of Presbyterian farmers. With the story itself based on real events, the author's detailed observations on local farming life and social attitudes are authentically, poignantly, rendered.

Stories of generational conflict are perhaps particularly interesting to the historian. The perennial battle between old and new, subtle shifts in social attitudes and beliefs, changes in lifestyle and in popular cultural activities over the relatively short term, are not easy to trace through conventional historical documents. Edmund Gosse's semi-fictional *Father and Son*, first published in 1907, is perhaps the classic example of this type of novel, and a particular favourite of mine, reflecting my interest in religious history – the novel deals with the late-Victorian crisis of faith in the context of a family of Plymouth Brethren. A few years ago, I was fortunate enough to be introduced to Max Wright's *Told in Gath* (1990), which, using Gosse's earlier novel as a kind of framework, describes with considerable skill and the personal insight of the deeply affected, his experience of Ulster fundamentalism:

> In Bangor, County Down, in the 1930s, we lived only half a mile away from the Tonic cinema, a pleasure dome entirely of its time, large by any standards and huge in provincial Bangor, the most sumptuous building in town. I passed it every day on my way to school, never failing to stop and examine the posters and the still photographs, drawn by the dreadful mystery of the place. My school friends talked excitedly about Gene Autry and Roy Rogers and Bud Abbott and Lou Costello but I realised that it could not be for me. Although I was seven years old and unsaved, and therefore bound for the same hell as the Saturday morning film fans if not, as the privileged child of many prayers, for one a great deal hotter, I knew better than to advance sophistically my worldling status as a reason for indulging in worldly practice. I recognised that it was my parents' duty to keep me unspotted from the world (James 1:27). As they were fond of remarking, you did not taste poison in order to test the strength so I sighed as a potential lover and consented as a dutiful son.[29]

In this novel, the local setting provides the backdrop for a more universal theme, the evocation of guilt aroused by the pressures of a strongly religious upbringing striking a chord with many of this author's generation. At the novel's close, Max Wright's reflections on the changes which have taken place over the course of his life, both within and outside the local Brethren community, reinforce the value of a narrative which in intent and achievement, matches that of Gosse: 'a document, a record of educational and religious conditions which, having passed away, will never return'.[30]

I am conscious of the very selective nature of this overview. The works I have discussed are those with which I have long been familiar and for which I have a personal preference; my interest in Ulster religious history has also been an important determining factor. To draw up a comprehensive list of authors, famous and forgotten, whose works would help shed light on past people and events would be a time-consuming, though not very difficult task. For those who wish to go further than the better-known writers, however, it would be both more advantageous, and more pleasant, to seek out your own examples. The local library or second-hand book shop can be the site of much happy and fruitful browsing, with the possibility of recovering a lost treasure providing an added incentive.

Today, works of fiction are clearly recognised as a valuable resource in reconstructing the past. Indeed, a growing number of scholarly works, books and journals and academic courses have been dedicated to just this type of interdisciplinary exercise. Reading a poem, short story or novel dealing with the time period and locality under investigation can provide a welcome respite from the perusal of more formal documents and, if treated with due seriousness and in combination with other documentary evidence, can provide considerable insight into 'the lived reality beneath the surviving facts'.[31]

1. Murray Kreiger, 'Fiction and historical reality: the hourglass and the sands of time' in *Literature and History*, xi (1985), p. 47.
2. Quoted in Geoffery Tillotson, *A view of Victorian literature* (Oxford, 1978), p. 47.
3. Benjamin Disraeli, *Sybil; or The Two Nations* (London, 1845).
4. *Fraser's Magazine* (January 1848), quoted in *Mary Barton: A tale of Manchester Life* ed. Stephen Gill (Harmondsworth, 1970), pp.15-16.
5. See for example, Geoffery Tillotson, *Mid-Victorian studies* (London, 1965); Kathleen Tillotson, *Novels of the 1840s* (Oxford, 1954); Elizabeth Jay, *The religion of the heart: Anglican evangelicalism and the nineteenth-century novel* (Oxford, 1979). For the later period, Robert Lee Wolff, *Gains and losses: novels of faith and doubt in Victorian England* (London, 1977).
6. Patrick Kavanagh, 'Epic' in *Patrick Kavanagh: Collected Works* (London, 1964).

7. Antoinette Quinn in Terence Brown and Nicholas Grene (eds), *Tradition and influence in Anglo-Irish poetry* (London, 1989).
8. D. H. Akenson and W. H. Crawford, *Local poets and social history: James Orr Bard of Ballycarry* (Belfast, 1977).
9. Akenson and Crawford, *Local poets and social history*, pp. 5-6.
10. Akenson and Crawford, *Local poets and social history*, p. 6.
11. Maria Edgeworth, *Castle Rackrent* (first published 1800, Oxford, 1995).
12. Kathryn Kirkpatrick, 'Introduction', *Castle Rackrent*, p. vii. For an analysis of Maria's work in a local context, Tom Dunne, 'A gentleman's estate should be a moral school' in Raymond Gillespie and Gerard Moran (eds), *Longford: Essays in county history* (Dublin, 1991).
13. Kirkpatrick, 'Introduction', pp. viii-ix.
14. Edgeworth, *Castle Rackrent*, pp. 13-14.
15. John Cronin, 'The nineteenth-century: a retrospect' in Augustine Martin (ed.), *The genius of Irish prose* (Dublin, 1985), p.11.
16. Sam Hanna Bell, 'William Carleton and his neighbours' in *Ulster Folklife vii* (1961), p. 37.
17. William Carleton, *Tales of Ireland* (1834), Introduction.
18. P. J. Murray in *Edinburgh Review* 1852, quoted in John Cronin, *The Anglo-Irish novel: volume i: the nineteenth century* (New Jersey, 1980), p. 90.
19. William Carleton, *The black prophet* (1847).
20. Cronin, *The Anglo-Irish novel*, p. 96.
21. 'If Carleton has no merit at all as a literary figure, he must surely hold a strong position as one of Ireland's preeminent social historians', Tess Hurson (ed.), *Inside the margins: a Carleton reader* (1992), p. 8; see also Maureen O'Rourke and James McKillop, *Irish literature, a reader* (Syracuse, 1987).
22. Cronin, *The Anglo-Irish novel*, pp. 88-98.
23. These extracts are taken from Anthony Trollope, *The Macdermots of Ballycloran*, (first published 1847, Oxford, 1989).
24. Anthony Trollope, cited in *The Macdermots of Ballycloran*, Introduction, p. viii.
25. See for example, J. Binns, *The miseries and beauties of Ireland* (2 vols London, 1837); T. C. Foster, *Letters on the condition of the people of Ireland* (London, 1846); J. Gamble, *Views of society and manners in the north of Ireland in the summer and autumn of 1812* (London, 1813); H. D. Inglis, *A journey throughout Ireland during the spring, summer and autumn of 1834*, 2 vols (London, 1835); J. G. Kohl, *Travels in Ireland* (London, 1844); B. Noel, *Notes of a short tour through the midland counties of Ireland in the summer of 1836* (London, 1837).
26. Anthony Trollope, *The Landleaguers* (first published 1883; Oxford, 1993), p. 261.
27. Mary Hamer, introduction to Trollope, *The Landleaguers*, p. xxii.
28. Jacqueline Ganet (ed.), *The Big House in Ireland: reality and representation* (Cork, 1991), p. xii, 17.

29. Max Wright, *Told in Gath* (Belfast, 1990), p.110.
30. Wright, *Told in Gath*, p.1.
31. Michael Wolff, 'Victorian Study: an interdisciplinary essay' in *Victorian Studies*, viii (1964), pp. 59-70. For studies which link literature with the wider theme of landscape, P. J. Duffy, 'Carleton, Kavanagh and the south Ulster landscape c. 1800–1950' *Irish Geography*, xviii (1985), pp. 25–37. P. J. Duffy 'Writing in Ireland: literature and art in the representation of Irish place' in Brian Graham (ed.), *In search of Ireland, A cultural geography* (London, 1997).

II

The practice of Irish local history

DOING LOCAL HISTORY: ARMAGH IN THE LATE EIGHTEENTH CENTURY

Leslie Clarkson

I

W. G. Hoskins, the doyen of English local history, was fond of quoting his favourite aphorism: 'to generalise is to be an idiot: to particularise is the alone distinction of merit'. With his colleagues in the Department of English Local History at the University of Leicester, he turned, 'the study of local history from an amateurish pot-pourri into a recognised academic discipline'. In the hands of Hoskins,

> specialised studies . . . are always used to illuminate and deepen our understanding of the wider aspects of demographic or agricultural history. He has shown that the more profound and thorough the local study, the more relevance it has for general history. Understanding is built up by a complex appreciation of local variety'.[1]

In Ireland, no less than in Britain, the lessons have been learnt. Local history thrives, and the national story is enriched.

History is important. We are what the past has made us; and what we believe the past to have been influences how we behave in the present. The purpose of doing history is to entertain, to instruct, and to enhance understanding of ourselves and the society of which we are part. Disquisitions on historical methodology are apt to be arid and are matters best left to be conducted between consenting adults in private. Nevertheless, I have been asked to write an 'how to do it' piece and this essay is about my approach to the study of the history of one town.

I have written 'doing history', not 'writing history', because writing is only one part of a four-stage process. The first is to have a reason for studying history. Curiosity is the best reason of all. A local historian, who is often, but by no means always, an amateur historian, may be driven by a desire to find out about 'my town'. For the professional, more interested, perhaps, in national themes, the motive might be the Hoskins' wish to enrich the general by a study of the particular. The second stage is the search for evidence. This is often the most exciting as one source leads to another. Then comes the difficult task of teasing out interpretations. The records of the past rarely wear their meanings on their sleeves. We need to ask why a document was written – or a picture drawn or photograph taken – and by whom. We have to decide whether we are extracting from the evidence information different from that which its creators intended. There are many tools available to the historian to assist him or her in the process of interpretation, but the most important is imagination, tempered by a respect for the evidence.

Finally, there is the stage of communication: talking, writing, or – more and more these days – exploiting the possibilities of the internet. Communication is important because history is a social activity. The pleasure of history is that it is a conversation: between the historian, his or her sources, and the audience. Like all good conversations the one influences the other. To illustrate all these stages, I describe how I came to write three articles about Armagh in the late eighteenth century and, with a colleague, a small book about one family living in the city.[2]

View of Armagh in 1810 by James Black. Reproduced courtesy of the Armagh County Museum.

II

Eighteenth-century Armagh was an ecclesiastical, administrative, post, and market town in south Ulster, with a population of no more than 2,000 in 1770. It stood at the centre of a prosperous linen-manufacturing district, and every Tuesday awakened to the sounds of weavers from the surrounding countryside and dealers from Dublin and elsewhere coming to buy and sell linen webs. From time to time judges, lawyers and litigants arrived, for Armagh was also an assize town. And as the primatial city of Ireland, Armagh thronged with resident and visiting clergy. The cathedral echoed with the anthems of Handel and slumbered to the dull drone of Primate Robinson's sermons.[3] I knew little of this when I was first attracted to Armagh in the 1970s. My concerns had been with English demographic history. It was demography that led me to Armagh and provided me with the initial spur to investigate its history further.

In 1770 the Rev. Dr William Lodge compiled 'A list of the inhabitants of the town of Armagh for the use of his Grace the Lord Primate'.[4] We cannot be sure of the archbishop's motives in ordering what was in effect a census of the population. Richard Robinson had been translated to the see of Armagh from Kildare in 1765 and, unlike his predecessors, chose to live in Armagh. He used his considerable wealth to grace the city with handsome buildings, including an episcopal palace, a chapel and a hospital. He was the town's largest landlord and he embarked on a programme of urban improvement by compelling his tenants to rebuild in limestone and slate. As head of the established church in Ireland he was clearly interested to know how many Anglicans, Presbyterians and Roman Catholics there were among his neighbours.

Archbishop Robinson did not 'enrich the republic of letters by any important works of his own composition', but he possessed an intellectual curiosity, common among men and women of his rank in the eighteenth century, that led him to build a library and an observatory, and provide new buildings for the classical school.[5] The compiler of the 1770 census of Armagh, the Rev. Dr William Lodge, was chancellor of the cathedral and Robinson's librarian. He was 'a man of extensive learning and considerable talents' and, like the archbishop, possessed of an inquiring mind.[6]

The eighteenth century was an age of statistics, not in the forbidding mathematical way that the word is used today, but in the older sense of 'numerical facts, systematically collected'. In 1745 the Physico-Historical Society of Ireland, under the direction of Walter Harris in Dublin, collected 'topographical and statistical returns' from correspondents throughout

Ireland, and in 1800 the Dublin Society commenced its county Statistical Surveys with the aid of a grant from the Dublin parliament.[7] William Lodge set about his task in 1770 in a similar spirit. He listed 499 households containing 1,948 people, distinguishing between husbands and wives, parents and children, and masters and servants. Lodge identified denominational allegiances and ascribed occupations.

Whatever purposes Lodge and the archbishop had in mind, here was a source that would tell us something about the size and structure of households in late eighteenth-century society. These were themes that were interesting demographers in the 1970s. Peter Laslett had argued that in England, and perhaps throughout western Europe, the small nuclear family was the norm from the sixteenth to the nineteenth century, and not the large extended family so beloved by sociologists.[8] Lodge's list might throw light on this question as well as illuminating economic activities in a busy Irish town.

Table 1: Households and denominations in Armagh, 1770

	Church of Ireland	Presbyterian	Roman Catholic	Whole population
Number and proportion of households	161 (32.3%)	130 (26. 1%)	208 (41.7%)	499 (100%)
Mean household size	4.12	3.90	3.81	3.93
Mean size of resident conjugal group.	3.69	3.80	3.77	3.75
Mean number of other kin, servants and lodgers	0.43	0.10	0.04	0.18
Proportion of households comprising parent(s) and child(ren)	49.4%	50.0%	58.8%	53.5%
Proportion of one-person households	17.3%	12.9%	8.8%	12.6%

The household and family structures of Armagh in 1770 are summarised in table one. Some comments are in order. First, we are using the census for much more than Lodge intended. At the end of his list he included his own summary: 162 'Church Families', 131 Presbyterian families, and 209 'Popish' families. The difference between these totals and those in table one is explained by the distinction between 'families' and 'households' which is discussed below. Second, Lodge reckoned the total population to be 1,880, made up of 900 'parents etc.' and 987 'children' (which does not add up to 1,880). The reason for the difference between his total and mine (1,948) is that Lodge did not include sixty-one domestic servants and apprentices who were recorded in a separate column in his census. Possibly he did not regard them as part of the town's population even though they lived there, more likely he simply forgot to add them on to the total. Lodge did all his counting in his head or on his fingers; there are running totals at the bottom of every page. The modern scholar can get the computer to do the sums.

Lodge made no attempt to calculate the average number of persons in a family and neither did he distinguish between 'families' and 'households'. This is a distinction invented by modern sociologists. The former refers to the conjugal family unit composed of parents and children; the latter includes also other kin, servants and lodgers living as part of the household. As we can see from table one, the average number of servants and others was four times greater in Church of Ireland households than in Presbyterian households, and ten times bigger than in Roman Catholic establishments. We can also see from table one that around a half of the households were nuclear in structure (that is, made up of families of parents and children). There was also a substantial proportion of houses containing only one person, particularly among the Church of Ireland population. The remaining households were enlarged by the presence of grandparents, grandchildren, uncles, aunts, or other kin. Armagh in 1770 does not support the assumption that extended family households were common place in Ireland.

These findings are of great interest. For two hundred years and more commentators on Ireland have assumed that households were large, but there has been little conclusive evidence one way or another.[9] The Armagh census points to an unexpectedly low figure, which raises the question of whether it was typical or untypical. This study of Armagh was done in the late 1970s. Since then a colleague and I have analysed a much more detailed census, that for Carrick-on-Suir, county Tipperary, taken in 1799. Carrick had many houses split into tenements and occupied by more than one household. In 1799 houses in Carrick contained, on average, 6.3 persons. The mean household size, however, was smaller, although 19 per cent greater than in Armagh (4.66 as compared to 3.93). This was because there were more resident kin in households in Carrick than in Armagh.[10] We might conclude, therefore, that Armagh in 1770 was not typical; or perhaps it was Carrick that was out of line. A more reasonable conclusion is that neither Armagh nor Carrick were representative of the whole of Ireland, but were part of a spectrum of household and family sizes. Both were urban communities and they may tell us nothing about the structure of families and households in rural communities. The only safe lesson to be learned is that we need more local studies. William Lodge noted occupations in Armagh, but he did not analyse his findings, beyond counting the number of public houses (was he worried about the amount of drunkenness?). He ascribed occupations to 471 people, that is fewer than 28 per cent of the population. This is a small proportion, but it does not mean that almost three-quarters of the population were not working. The explanation is that Lodge listed in a column headed 'trade' only the occupations of householders, but not those of their spouses and children unless they were different from those of the head of the household. But all family members, except the very young and very old, assisted the householder in his or her work. In the 'servant' column, Lodge noted the numbers of servants and apprentices (there were only five of the latter). Most servants were female and I have assumed that they were domestics, although possibly they helped in the family business as well.

Table 2: Distribution of occupations by industrial sector, Armagh, 1770

	Number	Percentage
Agricultural	2	0.4
Mining and quarrying	9	1.9
Building	14	2.9
Manufacturing	122	25.9
Transport	15	3.2
Dealing	116	24.6
Labouring	70	14.9
Public and professional service	49	10.3
Domestic and personal service	74	15.7
Total	471	99.9

Occupations in table two have been arranged according to an industrial classification devised in the late nineteenth century and modified in the twentieth.[11] Just as table one is based on some straightforward sociological concepts, so table two uses a very simple economic tool. We can sharpen the picture by enlarging the focus.

For example, included among the 122 manufacturers, were twenty-one workers in metal (blacksmiths, etc.), thirty-three workers in leather (shoemakers, saddlers, etc.), and twenty-four manufacturers of clothing (e.g. tailors). There were only nine linen workers, at most; Armagh was not a linen-making town although it was located within a linen-producing region. The largest groups in the dealing sector were the forty-nine drink sellers (Lodge had counted forty-eight), twenty-five shopkeepers and twenty food dealers (butchers, fruit dealers, mealmen, etc.). There were just five people living in Armagh who were involved with the buying and selling of linen.

The distinction between manufacturing and dealing is an artificial one in the eighteenth century since a shoemaker, say, was as likely to sell shoes as to make them. The professional people were mostly clergy, school teachers and government officials, such as hearth money collectors and gaugers. Workers in 'domestic and personal service' were principally living-in servants, although there was a sprinkling of out-servants, barbers and wig makers. The seventy labourers were general labourers about the town; many were probably building workers busily employed in the beautification of Armagh. They were all men and most were Roman Catholics.

In contrast to the unexpected picture of small household size in Armagh that emerges from table one, the occupational profile in table two is an unsurprising one. It is similar to that found in many small towns in western Europe during the eighteenth century. Both tables, nevertheless, tell us a great deal about Armagh and something about the economy and society of late eighteenth-century Ireland. Both have been extracted from a single document: Lodge's 'List of Inhabitants'. I have used as analytical tools simple sociology, simple economics, simple counting, simple computing, and a dash of imagination. Not every historian is formally acquainted with sociology or economics and not everyone has access to a computer, even a PC, which is all that is required. Everyone, though, has an imagination and everyone can count. Historians are sometimes reluctant to count, on the grounds that counting reduces the past to every figure except the human. But Dr Johnson recognised the advantages:

BOSWELL: Sir Alexander Dick tells me that he remembers having a
thousand people in a year to dine at his house.
JOHNSON: That, Sir, is about three a day.
BOSWELL: How your statement lessens the idea.
JOHNSON: That, Sir, is the good of counting. It brings everything to
a certainty, which before floated in the mind indefinitely.[12]

III

At this point my brief intellectual visit to Armagh might have ended. Like a package tourist, I had 'done Armagh' and it was time to move on. However, two happy chances caused me to dally. The first was an invitation to present a paper at a conference on the history of Irish towns. An enjoyable part of the historian's role is to communicate, so I accepted. But what to talk about? At the time many historians were interested in writing what the French call 'total history', that is, the complete history of a community. A classic example of the genre is Professor Le Roy Ladurie's study of the tiny French community of Montaillou in the early fourteenth century, based on an episcopal inquiry into heresy in the village.[13] He explored the economic and social background of the village, the structure of authority, and the beliefs of the inhabitants. The English historian and anthropologist, Alan Macfarlane, had recently published *Reconstructing historical communities*, a methodological handbook that drew on his experiences of studying English parishes in Essex and Cumbria in the seventeenth century, and on field work in Nepal. The publisher's blurb claimed, rather grandly, that 'for the amateur historian or genealogist who wants to know about a village or family, [Macfarlane's] method makes it possible to find out almost everything that survives in historical documents concerning each person who lived in a village, each plot of land and house'.[14]

A modest excursion into community history seemed to be worth trying. I had some idea of the social and economic structure of late eighteenth-century Armagh, and I had speculated on the motives of Archbishop Robinson and the Rev. Lodge in compiling the 1770 census. In the process I had used a splendid and near-contemporary local history, James Stuart's *Historical Memoirs of Armagh*, published in 1819. Stuart had been born and educated in Armagh, where his father had been a linen merchant. He was related to a long-established family in Armagh, the Ogles, one of whom, Thomas Ogle, constructed the street in the town in 1759 that bears his name. Stuart's *Historical Memoirs* contain a wealth of gossipy information about many of the families who feature on the list of inhabitants. There were other sources too: the corporation book for the period 1738-1818, in the Armagh Public Library (APL) which showed how the grand jury governed Armagh; the (incomplete) Church of Ireland parish registers from the 1750s to the 1780s in the Public Record Office of Northern Ireland (PRONI); leases among the estate papers of archbishops and other landholders in the APL and PRONI; occasional references (usually advertisements) in the *Belfast News-Letter* and in the Journals of the Irish House of Commons; and Charles Coote's *Statistical survey of county Armagh*.[15]

The conference paper attempted to do four things. First it tried to locate a sense of community in eighteenth-century Armagh – not an easy thing to do, since sociologists have offered nearly one hundred definitions of community.[16] Second, it argued that, despite the obvious differences in economic positions, wealth and religious beliefs, there was a set of values shared by the citizens of Armagh. These values stemmed from the functions of the city as a centre of trade, production, consumption, administration and entertainment. Third, it tried to uncover kinship links between households as well as within them. Did married sons and daughters live in the house next to their

parents or in a house in the street round the corner? Many of these neigh-
bourly connections were found to be present, re-enforcing the sense of community. Finally, it posed the question: was the population of Armagh stable,
or did people move in and out like migrant workers in a frontier town? The
answer to this question was that there was a small core of families that had
been in Armagh for a long time, from the early seventeenth century in some
cases, but the majority of families whom Lodge recorded in 1770 had not
been there very long.

The outcome of this venture into community history did not satisfy
everyone. One reviewer of the published version of the essay dismissed it as
'disappointing', based on 'outdated' sociology, thin evidence, and reaching
'conclusions that are too speculative at this stage'.[17] The sociological model
was certainly wellworn, although not clapped-out, and the evidence was well
strained, but had not, I think, snapped. As to 'speculative', I plead guilty. The
paper was a *ballon d'essai*, an attempt to squeeze as much information as possible out of a limited stock of information with the aid of a few concepts and
rather more imagination.

IV

The second happy chance that extended my stay in Armagh, was the discovery of 'an inventory of the Goods Assetts and Effects of the late Mrs.
Annaritta Cust taken by the Direction of the Executors viz. the Rev. Thomas
English, The Rev. John Mee, Joshua McGeough and Robert Livingston
Esq.'[18] The inventory was taken in December, 1797. Twenty-seven years earlier, William Lodge had listed as living in Market Street, the most prominent
street in Armagh, 'Misses Custs, three sisters'. There was no other information, except that they were members of the established church. Was
Annaritta Cust one of the sisters? The prefix 'Mrs' was initially confusing,
until I realised that it was a courtesy title sometimes accorded in the eighteenth century to unmarried ladies of advanced years. The lady in question
was indeed the last surviving of the three sisters; there was also a fourth, married, sister, and a brother.

The inventory is a remarkable document.[19] For seven days Miss Cust's
executors moved through eighteen rooms in a three-storey house, peering
into cupboards, crawling under stairs, rummaging through drawers, and
itemising the personal effects, not of one individual, but of five or six members of a close-knit and long-lived family. A lady whose possessions included
clothes in profusion, maps of the world and of county Tyrone, busts of relations, books and pictures galore, gloves, gaming boards and mathematical

instruments, silver coffee pots and cracked tea pots, wine bottles – full and empty – patent medicines, a parrot's cage, and 'two asses . . . of an Advanced Age No body remembers how old they are Long hooves & short thighs', was a lady worth knowing.

If the totalling of households and occupations in section II was the product of arithmetic, and the community links in section III the creation of speculation, the quest for Annaritta Cust is the story of the historian turned detective. The trail led us from Armagh, to Belfast, to Dublin, to London and to Lincolnshire. It even took us into the Armagh countryside in a fruitless search for the burial place of the Custs.[20] In addition to the familiar sources – Lodge' s list, Stuart's *Memoirs*, and Annaritta's inventory – we became acquainted with family and estate papers, particularly those of the Cust relations, the Burges's, deposited in PRONI, copies of deeds, leases and marriage settlements lodged in the Registry of Deeds in Dublin, and the letter books of the Irish customs commissioners at the Public Record Office in London.[21]

Miss Cust proved elusive. The difficulty with pursuing women through history is that they leave so few traces. They change their surnames on marriage and often their Christian names are lost as well. When William Lodge recorded the inhabitants of Armagh he noted the Christian names of only twenty-one females, out of a total of nearly one thousand. Women rarely followed occupations in their own right or took out leases, or held public office. The discipline of women's history that has developed during the last two decades has been inspired, in part, by a determination to recover the history of the forgotten half of human kind. The search for Annaritta Cust was a modest foray into this genre of history.

Fortunately, the name Cust is sufficiently singular to stand out and for us to assume that any other Cust we came across was likely to be related in some way to Annaritta Cust. The assumption proved correct. In 1767 Richard Livingston drew a plan of Armagh for the archbishop that showed a Mr Cust holding property in several parts of the city. There was a Henry Cust who served as high sheriff of the county of Armagh in 1769 and a Henry Cust who was a member of the city grand jury and sovereign of Armagh on nine occasions. It was highly likely that he was a brother, or a cousin, or even Annaritta's father. If we could not find the lady, perhaps we could find the man and learn something about Annaritta and her sisters in the process.

There turned out to be two Henry Custs, one Annaritta's grandfather and the other her brother. The first was born around 1650, possibly in Lincolnshire. He probably came to Ireland after the Restoration at a time when many younger sons of English gentlemen found Ireland an attractive place: there was land to be acquired cheaply and employment to be had in government service. Henry Cust the grandfather lived briefly in Armagh, but was in Derry during the siege and then moved to Sligo where he held a minor post in the Irish customs service. He also rented land from the bishop of Derry in the Magilligan area.

The first Henry Cust died in 1717. He had two sons, one of whom, Jones, settled in Armagh in 1712. Jones (sometimes written Jonas) was the father of Annaritta Cust and her two unmarried sisters, Margaret and Judith, and also of another daughter, Elizabeth, who married the Rev. Dr David Burges of Dublin and Armagh. He was also the father of the second Henry Cust. Jones was employed by the Irish revenue service as a collector of excise duties in county Armagh. He was also a barrack master responsible for the maintenance of military barracks in county Armagh. Excise duties on beer, whiskey and ale houses were major sources of revenue for the Dublin administration during the eighteenth century and a great deal of money passed through the hands of the collectors. The Barrack Board and Board of Works were responsible for the upkeep of military establishments and government buildings. They have been described as 'an organization that dwarfed any contemporary business concern'.[22] Jones Cust was a busy man, trusted and well respected by the Dublin establishment. He died in Dublin in 1754 whilst visiting on government business.

The second Henry Cust was born in 1707 and died in 1781. Like his father before him, he held government office as a collector of excise duties for county Armagh and barrack master; he took over the post of collector from his father in 1738 and shared the duties of barrack master with his father for a time. Henry invested shrewdly in land during the 1750s, mostly by taking leases from the archbishopric of Armagh at low rents and modest entry fines, and sub-letting the land in small farms at rack rents. He financed some of his land dealings with government monies that he retained by delaying the settling of his accounts with his superiors in Dublin, a practice for which he was almost dismissed and which eventually compelled his resignation. Dublin gossip in the early 1770s suggests that Henry may also have married an heiress and that the marriage was not a happy one. By one means or another he became a wealthy man and built a handsome house at Ballynahone, a mile or so from Armagh. He moved back into the city shortly before his death, possibly to live with his unmarried sisters. The path that led from Annaritta's inventory ran rich indeed.

What did we learn on the journey? Not a great deal about Annaritta Cust, it must be admitted, although more, perhaps, than we expected. When she died she was well into her eighties and was the sole surviving member of a family that had been in Armagh since at least 1712. Annaritta Cust was probably born in Armagh and lived out her whole life in the city. She was, nevertheless, a woman of wide interests, as the maps and books in her house testify. If her intellectual tastes were catholic, her faith was strongly Protestant and she left money in her will for the support of Protestant orphans. She was wealthy or, at any rate, had accumulated wealth over the years as she inherited the property of her siblings. She was a hoarder, even by the standards of the eighteenth century, when few things were thrown away but were turned to practical use, however decrepit they might appear.[23] The paraphernalia listed on her inventory included the worldly possessions of Henry and Judith and Margaret, and perhaps Jones also, as well as those of Annaritta herself. Over the years they had settled in corners and cupboards, parlours and pantries, like so much geological sediment. The inventory, unfortunately, does not record valuations – save for a few items – and the surviving version is probably a working draft. Nevertheless it reveals a cultured, comfortable, cluttered, but prosperous life, blighted at the end by old age and loneliness.[24]

If the glimpses of Miss Annaritta Cust are tantalizing, the picture of the male Custs, and particularly the younger Henry, is more substantial. Henry the elder, Jones Cust, and Henry the younger, were variously collectors of customs and excise duties, and barrack masters. Revenue officers are familiar figures in Irish literature, caricatured by Maria Edgeworth, vilified by Trollope, and treated more soberly by Professor K. H. Connell.[25] But the correspondence between the Revenue Board in Dublin, and Jones and Henry Cust the younger in Armagh, reveals an efficient and well-structured bureaucracy. When Henry was seriously in arrears with his accounts in the late 1750s, his Dublin masters pursued him with vigour. The Barrack Board and Board of Works were less well conducted and were notorious for their corrupt practices. Both Jones and Henry over-charged the Board for work done to the buildings for which they were responsible.

In his land dealings, Henry Cust was an example of that important class in eighteenth-century society: the middleman. Like revenue officers, middlemen are among the villains of pre-Famine society, although there have been attempts to rehabilitate them.[26] Henry Cust rented land and sub-let to tenant farmers. At one stage in his career, in the early 1760s, he overstretched himself, causing his widowed mother and unmarried sisters who seem to have depended on him, some financial embarrassment. Nevertheless, he survived and grew rich. His outgoings in head rents and other charges were considerably less than the rents he received from his sub-tenants. The farms he let were improved and, in the case of those at Ballynahone Mor, enjoyed good communications with the markets in Armagh. Henry was a long-serving member of the grand jury that governed Armagh, and he ensured that the roads and bridges between the town and his properties were maintained in good order.

Henry Cust the first was probably an impoverished younger son of an English gentry family. Henry Cust the second had become an Anglo-Irish gentleman. His sphere of influence was provincial Ireland, not Dublin, although he had powerful supporters in the capital. As high sheriff for county Armagh he was responsible for the organization of elections and of the legal assizes; he would not have been appointed had he not been acceptable to the Dublin authorities. He may have died in the house of his sister Annaritta; certainly many of his 'goods assetts and effects' were among her possessions when she died in 1797. Indirectly, the quest for Miss Cust of Armagh has illuminated the workings of the Irish public finances, the behaviour of middlemen, and the mechanisms of local government. It has also, obliquely, thrown a little light on the position of women in eighteenth-century society.

V

Now to the final stage, that of writing. Even in these days of electronic communication, the written word remains the most important way of bringing the past to the attention of the present. Writing is the most personal and difficult part of doing history. 'If historians thought that their labours involved nothing but research, they would lead easier lives', Professor G. R. Elton has written. 'Honest and thorough research [he continued] can be exhausting and tedious. But honest and thorough writing will certainly be those things, and the agony of forcing thought into order and pattern should not be despised'. This sounds like a counsel of despair, particularly when he added, 'in a very real sense history cannot be correctly written'.[27]

Still writing must be done, and for two reasons. The first is that identified by Professor Elton: 'forcing thought into order and pattern'. It is only when we come to write that we begin to distinguish between what we know, what we think we know, and what we still need to know. Writing requires us to think about our information. For that reason it is good practice for writing and research to proceed hand-in-hand. Too many historians try to collect first and then to write. The result is an incomprehensible morass of material and writing is forever delayed until the document that explains all turns up – it never does. The second reason is that writing completes the loop between the past, the historian, and the present. Finding out about the past is fun; writing is hard; communicating is important. And the chief means of communication is writing.

Because writing is a personal matter, I hesitate to offer any general advice, but there are three principles to which all historians should adhere. The first is: be true to the past. Bring to the evidence all the interpretative tools that can be mustered, including imagination. But do not push interpretations beyond the point that the evidence can justify. Above all, do not distort the facts to accommodate prejudice. That way lies disaster. 'Good history', wrote the distinguished historian Richard Pares, 'cannot do so much service as money or science, but bad history can do almost as much harm as the most disastrous scientific discovery in the world'.[28] Bad history is always the result of distortion.

The second rule is: avoid patronising either the past or the present. People in the past were not quaint, nor simple and they should not be regarded as such. They possessed value systems different from our own, and our task as historians is to understand those systems. Do not write 'listen-with-mother' history, but treat your audience with respect. Whether it is made up of children or adults, amateurs or professionals, it should be taken seriously, which is not the same as saying that it should be addressed without humour.

Finally, write clearly, directly and grammatically. Sloppy writing betrays sloppy thinking. Avoid jargon, but do not confuse jargon with legitimate technical terms. Be clear about causes and effects; this is usually best achieved by writing in the active voice rather than the passive. Words ending in '-ism' and '-ology' are best avoided. Professor T. S. Ashton once recalled, on the eve of the publication of an elegantly written book about eighteenth-century England, 'I boasted that no single word ending in "ism" would be found in this book. 'Not even "baptism"?' asked one of my hosts . . . The proofs had not yet been returned to the publisher: it would have been easy to substitute "christening"; but I decided to leave the offensive syllables as a warning to myself against vainglory'.[29]

In the earlier sections of this essay I outlined my own eclectic approach to writing about Armagh in the eighteenth century. I offer no recipe for doing local history, except that the starting point should be a desire to find out about the past because the past is important. But I may have demonstrated something of the fugue between the local and the general that is the characteristic of the Hoskins approach to local studies. Ultimately the best local history ceases to be local and becomes general history.

1. C. W. Chalklin and M. A. Havinden (eds), *Rural change and urban growth 1500-1800: essays in English regional history in honour of W. G. Hoskins* (London, 1974), pp. ix-x.

2. L. A. Clarkson, 'An anatomy of an Irish town: the economy of Armagh, 1770' in *Irish Economic and Social History*, v (1978); L. A. Clarkson, 'Household and family structure in Armagh city, 1770' in *Local Population Studies*, xx (1978); L. A. Clarkson, 'Portrait of an urban community: Armagh 1770' in D. W. Harkness and Mary M O'Dowd (eds), *The town in Ireland: Historical Studies*, XIII (Belfast, 1981); L. A. Clarkson and E. Margaret Crawford, *Ways to wealth: The Cust family of eighteenth-century Armagh* (Belfast, 1985).

3. 'The sermons, which he [Archbishop Richard Robinson] sometimes preached, were both in style and in doctrine most excellent – but his voice was low and indistinctly heard.' James Stuart, *Historical memoirs of the city of Armagh. for a period of 1373 years . . .* (Newry, 1819), p. 454.

4. Armagh Public Library, G/5/20. There is an imperfect typescript copy in Public Record Office of Northern Ireland [hereafter PRONI], T 1288. Dr W. H. Crawford, then of the PRONI, first brought the document to my attention.

5. Stuart, *Armagh* pp. 444-54.

6. Stuart, *Armagh* p. 538.

7. The papers of the Physico-Historical Society are in the Armagh Public Library, Lodge Mss, 35. For an account of the statistical surveys see James Meenan and Desmond Clarke (ed.), *The Royal Dublin Society, 1731-1981* (Dublin, 1981), pp. 20-2.

8. Peter Laslett (ed.), *Household and family in past time* (Cambridge, 1972), chapters 1 and 4.

9. K. H. Connell, *The population of Ireland 1750-1845* (Oxford, 1950), pp. 17-26; F. J. Carney, 'Aspects of pre-famine Irish household size; composition and differentials', in L. M. Cullen and T. C. Smout (eds), *Comparative aspects of Scottish and Irish economic and social history 1600-1900,* (Edinburgh, 1974), pp. 32-46; L. A. Clarkson, 'Irish population revisited, 1687-1821', in J. M. Goldstrom and L. A. Clarkson (eds), *Irish population, economy. and society: essays in honour of the late K. H. Connell* (Oxford, 1981), pp. 18-25.

10. L. A. Clarkson, 'The demography of Carrick-on-Suir, 1799' in *Proceedings of the Royal Irish Academy*, xxxvii, section C, no. 2 (1987), pp. 2-36.

11. W. A. Armstrong, 'The use of information about occupation' in E. A. Wrigley (ed.), *Nineteenth-century society* (Cambridge, 1971), pp. 228-30.

12. Quoted in D. N. McCloskey, *Econometric history* (London, 1987), p. 42.

13. Emmanuel Le Roy Ladurie, *Montaillou: Cathars and Catholics in a French village 1294-1324* (London, 1978).

14. Alan Macfarlane, *Reconstructing historical communities* (Cambridge, 1977).

15. Sir Charles Coote, *Statistical survey of the county of Armagh* (Dublin, 1804).

16. Macfarlane, *Reconstructing historical communities*, p. 2.

17. Alan Rogers, reviewing Harkness and O'Dowd (ed.), *The town in Ireland*, in *Irish Economic and Social History*, ix (1982), p. 97.
18. PRONI, D288/134. This is a typescript copy. The original is among the papers of Y. A. Burges, PRONI, T1007. The word 'discovery' is perhaps rather strong. As with the list of inhabitants, Dr W. H. Crawford drew my attention to the inventory.
19. It is printed in full in Clarkson and Crawford, *Ways to wealth*, pp. 67-82.
20. The 'we' includes my colleague and co-author of *Ways to wealth*, Dr E. M. Crawford. The inquiries in Lincolnshire were purely by post.
21. The sources are listed in detail in Clarkson and Crawford, *Ways to wealth*, pp. 83-8.
22. R. B. McDowell, *Ireland in the age of imperialism and revolution. 1760-1801* (Oxford, 1979), p. 102.
23. On this point see, Donald Woodward, ' "Swords into ploughshares": recycling in pre-industrial England' in *Economic History Review*, second series, xxxviii (1985), pp. 175-91.
24. All these matters are elaborated in Clarkson and Crawford, *Ways to wealth*.
25. K. H. Connell, 'Illicit distillation' in K. H. Connell, *Irish peasant society: four historical essays* (Oxford, 1968), pp. 1-50. There is an absurd, brief, description of an encounter with a guager in Maria Edgeworth's *The Absentee* (1812). Captain Myles Usher, a revenue officer is the villain of Anthony Trollope's *The MacDermots of Ballycloran* (1847).
26. David Dickson, 'Middlemen', in Thomas Bartlett, D. W. Hayton (eds), *Penal era and golden age* (Belfast, 1979), pp. 162-85.
27. G. R. Elton, *The practice of history* (London, 1969), pp. 114, 115. For some helpful hints on writing David Dymond, *Writing local history* (Chichester, 1988).
28. Richard Pares, 'The revolt against colonialism' in R. A. and Elizabeth Humphreys (eds), *The historian's business and other essays* (Oxford, 1961), p. 68.
29. T. S. Ashton, *An economic history of England: the eighteenth century* (London, 1955), p. v.

THE STUDY OF TOWNLANDS IN ULSTER

W. H. Crawford

Irish people are aware of the significance of that measure of land known as the 'townland'. Many of them are proud to have their surnames identified with the name of their own townlands. They have been brought up to appreciate its traditions and its special character and so they can intrigue and entertain visitors with tales about its secret places and about the folk who have inhabited it. This information is often referred to as 'folklore' and its interpretation is often seen as the preserve of academics. Local historians, however, believe that all of us should be enabled to interpret the history of our townlands. They are beginning to realise that it is possible to enhance local knowledge and tradition by combining it with documentary evidence for each and every townland in the archives of the Ordnance Survey, the Valuation Office, and the Census Office. Their comprehensive coverage of all Ireland enables us to construct an approach to local studies that can be applied to the whole country. In Ulster much of this material is already available in the Public Record Office of Northern Ireland (PRONI) and the several major libraries of the province where it can be supplemented by modern sources such as newspapers. In the Republic the National Archives, the Valuation Office and the county libraries fulfil the same role.

It has to be said that academic historians have been too quick to condemn parish pump history. They have argued that it is too concerned with trivial detail to interest any but local people, and that it also lacks any sense of historical perspective. Over the years, however, I have realised that much of the gossip that I have heard about communities contained material of real significance for social historians, and that it could be used to understand the historical character of those individual communities, especially when married to existing documentary sources. Our purpose is to relate these sources to the particular interests and knowledge of local people, the study of the townland or group of townlands that they know well. While genealogists focus on indi-

vidual families, local historians study communities and so we need to empha-
sise that we intend to concentrate our study on the history of the community
that inhabited the townland or group of townlands, and to ensure that its
experience is placed in historical perspective. Such research studies should
enable us to tap wells of historical experience for fresh information that can
be collected, analysed and processed to provide a more accurate and detailed
understanding of our past. It will make us more aware of factors that have not
been properly appreciated and help us to assess their significance. The purpose of this paper is to suggest how we might go about creating the historical perspective that should inform this investigation and provide guidance
for students about the sources they can consult and the issues they should
address.

Certain topics jump to mind, such as population growth and decline, the
impact of emigration, changing farming practices, and housing for instance.
Other, less obvious, topics include the creation of farms after the English
system of estates was introduced in the early seventeenth century, the development of the road network opening up the vast tracts of hill-country to settlement and to the penetration of the market, and the roles played by
churches and schools in creating and modernising communities. There are
other topics about which we know little or nothing, such as the interference
of the law in everyday matters as well as relations between landlords and tenants, between tenants themselves, or between tenants and cottiers, affected
as they all were by a very lively land market. We have to consider how the
inhabitants of each of our chosen townlands reacted to all these pressures and
why their response differed from place to place.

I

For all practical purposes the starting date for most studies should be the
present and we should begin with a close and thorough examination of the
district using the latest edition of the Ordnance Survey map. If working
copies are prepared from it, they can be annotated and coloured in their turn
to present the research findings. We can use these working copies, for example, to record significant changes between the successive editions of the six
inch to the mile Ordnance Survey maps (held in the Public Record Office of
Northern Ireland or county libraries in the Republic). Because the first edition of the maps for Ulster made in the 1830s does not contain field boundaries, it is wiser to concentrate instead on the revised map made in the late
1850s and early 1860s, a superb example of the mapmaker's art. An
unmarked copy of it should be kept for the production of xerox copies. On to

the first of the xerox copies should be transcribed the boundaries of farm-holdings and locations of buildings *c.*1860 as recorded on the maps accompanying the Griffith valuation, because these maps contain the first ever comprehensive coverage of such information for the whole island of Ireland. When this has been completed for the townland it is worthwhile to transcribe the information given on the same sheet number of the First Valuation done in the 1830s. On this Valuation map, however, the townland was divided not into holdings but into convenient areas whose land quality could be described and assessed for valuation by the valuation officers. These valuation maps for Northern Ireland are held in PRONI (VAL 12D and VAL 1A respectively), and those for the Republic are in the Valuation Office, Dublin and the Field Books in the National Archives.

Various questions arise from the initial study of the map. The most obvious relate to the boundary of each townland in terms of its neighbours. From the Bodley maps of 1609-10 we should be able to note whether or not the townland under review existed as an independent entity at the time of the Plantation. If it did not, then we need to search for the first mention of it, at first in estate documents such as patents and leases, and then in the Down Survey of the mid-1650s, the 'census' of 1659, and the hearth-money and poll tax returns of the 1660s. Are we looking at townlands in the vicinity of the landlord's house that were colonised by British settlers in the early years of the Plantation, or at more extensive and remote districts of marginal land that had yet to be divided? We need to consider the relationship that any new townland might have had to its predecessor. The history of townlands and their creation may be more complex than we have reckoned and it may differ from region to region throughout the whole country.

Once we have established the date of the original townland boundary, we need to trace it out on the ground to find out how it was defined. Very often the boundary followed the line of a stream but elsewhere it usually had to be constructed or defined. Seventeenth-century leases indicate that tenants were often required to 'mear and ditch the outbounds and plant them with whitethorn quicksets'. Timber trees such as sycamore, ash, holly or crab-apple, were planted on these ditches. Where stones had to be cleared from the land the obvious solution was to build stone walls. In boggy or marshy ground an early practice was to define the boundary with 'mearing stones'. There are many references in estate papers to the settlement of boundary disputes by consulting the oldest inhabitants.

After settling the mearings we can begin to consider how the original townland was subdivided into compact farms, each with its own farmhouse. Often these early farms corresponded with natural sub-divisions of the townland. Leases refer sometimes to 'quarters' and occasionally to 'islands' of arable land in the bogs. These sub-denominations are more likely to be discovered on surviving estate maps than on Ordnance Survey maps. Nevertheless, because most of these farms, in their turn, became sub-divided into even smaller holdings, it is often possible to determine the original boundaries. There is no substitute for examining the mearings and fences on the ground!

Sub-division created other problems. One of the most important for any farmer was access from his farm to a main road, referred to in law as 'a right of way'. The range of solutions devised to solve this problem has left its mark on the landscape, ranging from the maze of narrow lanes picking up cottage after cottage in the densely-populated fine-linen weaving countryside of north Armagh, to the spur lanes running off main roads to the several farmsteads along their routes in county Antrim, or the long loanings climbing up to the last cottage in the marginal lands of the Sperrins. And, of course, the construction of a new road could mean the re-orientation of the rights-of-way. In short, it can be well worthwhile to take a second look at the roads and lanes in each townland.

The location of ancient churches, monasteries, castles, and other older monuments on the map should remind us that every townland had a history before the Plantation. It is essential, therefore, to visit the reading-room at the Environment and Heritage Service, described in Nick Brannon's essay below, or the Archaeological Survey at the Office of Public Works for the Republic, and mark up on your xeroxed map the location of each of the field monuments in the townland. Information will be available about some of the sites and, if you know of others, you can add to the official record. Although such source materials may be scarce, we have to use them in conjunction with geography and archaeology in order to realise some concept of the heritage of the district. Look through J. P. Mallory & T. E. McNeill's *The Archaeology of Ulster* (1991)[1] and the published volumes of the Northern Ireland Place-Names Project (based in the Department of Celtic Studies at Queen's University, Belfast) for potential approaches. Very valuable, too, in understanding the changing structure of Ulster society at that time is Katharine Simms, *From Kings to Warlords* (1987).[2]

II

Townlands cannot be studied in isolation especially after they became components of the new estates that were created throughout Ulster during the reign of James I. Although, at the outset, several adventurers managed to get large estates for themselves in the counties of Antrim and Down (while Monaghan for a time remained largely in the hands of its Irish owners), the remaining six counties in Ulster were confiscated by the crown after the flight of the earls in 1607 and reallocated to new owners. Because there were no proper surveys of the confiscated counties, the crown had to adapt the existing Irish measurements of townlands. These were then sketched out roughly on the basis of evidence provided by native juries: these maps have survived and are known to students as the Bodley maps. Their history is explained by J. H. Andrews.[3] The new estates were based on these maps. The government's plans ensured that they would be much less extensive than those in Antrim and Down but, like them, they were compact and many of them were large enough to sustain an estate town.

In the Plantation project it has often been overlooked that the crown was insisting that every landowner had to lease the bulk of his estate to tenants who would hold their lands according to any of the forms of tenure then current in England. The landowner was therefore not at liberty to treat his estate as a ranch, but was required to attract tenants to inhabit it. If he wished to profit from his lands, the landowner had to negotiate the terms of leases with potential tenants and then help them to make a success of their holdings so that they could pay money rents. The government enforced this provision by sending round commissioners on four occasions between 1610 and 1622; among other things they inquired about the nature of the tenancies that had been granted.

Although the new landlords might have preferred to make minimum concessions, they were forced by a shortage of potential tenants to offer good terms and even, in their absence, to offer leases to Irishmen. After 1628[4] many of the landlords were prepared to take out new patents and pay an increased rent to the crown for permission to lease up to a quarter of their individual estates to Irishmen. As a result, the practice of granting leases was widely established in Ulster from Plantation times. Every landlord wanted tenants who could afford to pay rents regularly (even if they had to be extracted from them in the courts as debts), to develop their holdings by fencing the outbounds and erecting a dwelling-house, and to carry out the covenants in the leases. Would-be tenants appreciated the value of a lease in terms of security of tenure as well as security for loans and mortgages: at the same time, however, they were well aware of the obligations that they would be incurring. In the event those who failed usually ran away.

In these leases the basic unit of measurement was the townland, although contemporaries recognised that the majority of townlands contained subdi-

Part of the Down Survey of Co. Meath, Sir William Petty, c. 1657, an early map showing townlands.

visions with names of their own: sometimes these subdivisions became townlands in their own right. In the more remote districts a substantial tenant might obtain several townlands, but near the towns he would be fortunate to get a single townland. Especially in the early years of the Plantation, landlords valued such substantial tenants highly because they were potential allies, or at least assistants, in organising and administering an estate. Where this was the case, these 'freeholds' remained a rare but important feature of the countryside.

Elsewhere, over succeeding generations, townlands fractured into smaller but still compact farms. The timing, extent, and nature of this process depended to a great extent on the leasing policies of landlords, although their decisions were often responses to changes in the wider community.[5] The primary instinct of a tenant was to preserve his farm intact for the next generation, but in most families children would insist on sub-dividing it after his death. If the father was intent on preserving the home farm by leaving it intact to his eldest son, he could satisfy the other children only by endowing them with money, purchasing other farms, or setting them up in trade, commerce, or a profession. Even in the seventeenth century there was a busy land market which landlords tried to control by insisting that they had to approve the transactions.

Another instinct of a tenant was to take on under-tenants who would pay their rents to him in cash, work, or kind. Whenever land was in great demand the tenant often decided that sub-letting parts of his farm, especially the outskirts, was more profitable than farming it. He had to be careful, however, not to provide the sub-tenant with a permanent claim to the holding. If he did, the landlord could argue that the tenant was giving up his tenant-right of the piece of land he had sublet, so that when the lease came up for renewal this landlord could decide to let the holding directly to the prosperous sub-tenant, thus converting him into a leaseholder. As a result, many farms were split into much smaller farms whenever leases came up for renewal. By 1800, for example, it was reckoned that the average size of farms in the linen county of Armagh was less than ten acres. Elsewhere in Ulster it would appear that farmers managed to prevent this from happening and retained their farms. In such circumstances sub-tenants became merely cottiers who held their smallholdings or 'cottakes' at the whim of the farmer. Travellers through the lowlands of Ulster in the mid nineteenth century saw a landscape of dispersed farms with attendant cottier houses and smallholdings, all heavily cultivated.

Indeed, the patterns of fields on the lowland farms with their hawthorn (whitethorn) hedgerows contrasted markedly with the extensive townlands of the uplands, where houses tended to cluster on patches of good land and fences were walls of stone cleared from the fields. There, men of some substance, who had secured leases from their landlords for one or more townlands, had acted as middlemen by setting farms to poorer men. The middlemen were not prepared to grant leases to these poorer men because that would have given them some security of tenure: here, too, the middlemen feared that the landlord might seize a suitable opportunity such as the renewal of the 'head' or main lease to let such farms directly to the occupiers. In time, however, this class of middlemen was forced out by a combination of landlords and farmers. On some other estates landlords leased farms to groups of partners, making each of the partners jointly responsible for payment of the rent: if one of the farmers could not pay his rent, the other partners were still liable for the whole rent. Within the framework of such a lease families, partners, or kin-groups organised the collection of rent and allocated land. This practice became known as 'rundale' and it displayed infinite variations because, in the absence of legal adjudicators, participants made arrangements to suit circumstances. Its major asset was flexibility that often suited short-term situations, such as the aftermath of a death in the family. In the longer term, however, it was likely to lead to bad blood among the parties. For this reason it was viewed as a major obstacle in the long term to the introduction of improved farming practices that were necessary to exploit the commercial markets expanding throughout the province. It often proved difficult for partners to make permanent divisions of land that had been held in partnership unless the owner of the estate or his agent was prepared to intervene to supervise and underwrite the transaction. Even after permanent field boundaries were defined, the practice of holding the mountain grazing in common continued, and even today every farmer knows how many 'soums' (units of grazing) he can claim there: by the middle of the nineteenth century the valuation of soums appears in the manuscript books of Griffith's Valuation.[6]

By the early nineteenth century, Ulster was fast becoming the province of the small tenant farmer. This trend was further accentuated by the decline of the hand-spinning of linen yarn and, later in the century, by the collapse of handloom-weaving in many parts of the province. As fewer farmers were able to supplement their farm incomes by domestic industry, they had to farm more intensively on farms that were the smallest in Western Europe. In contrast with the easing of landlord-tenant relations during the growing prosperity of the eighteenth century, the nineteenth century witnessed the increasing tension between landlord and tenant that became known as the 'land question'. In the thirty years that succeeded the Famine the landlords were successful in their struggle to maintain their legal rights, but the Land Acts of 1870 and 1881, and the beginning of a long recession in agriculture, undermined their determination.

> By 1914 three-quarters of occupiers were buying out their landlords, mostly under the great acts of 1903 and 1904, which directly initiated the decisive decline of tenancy and led to the transfer in ownership of about nine million acres to the occupiers. In the 1920s, in both parts of Ireland, land purchase was made compulsory and the remaining tenanted land was taken from the landlords. The most striking sign of the decline of land-lordism, the disappearance of the gentry from the countryside, was only evident from that decade: by the 1970s hardly one quarter of the mansion houses of the 1870s were lived in by the descendants of nineteenth-century landed families.[7]

To discover when and how this major change in landownership was implemented in your district, consult the Valuation Revision manuscript books in PRONI (VAL12B) or in the Valuation Office in Dublin. This can be checked with the archives of the Irish Land Commission and the Land Registry, which is especially useful for the many tiny estates that had been created by families over the previous two and a half centuries. Less typical, but of more value, are the surviving records of the great estates because they were administered by professional staff. Some of them contain illuminating correspondence about the sales!

When the ownership of land passed from landlords to farmers an old device reappeared in a new guise. Whereas the estate office had been responsible for confirming a tenant's title to his land, the new owners had to protect their own rights with the paid help of solicitors. How could they lease any of their newly-acquired land to another farmer without running the risk of losing their title to it? To solve the problem they resurrected the concept of 'conacre'. Before the Famine conacre was related mainly to agreements made between farmers and cottiers: in return for the farmer's permission to plant a crop of potatoes on his land, the cottier agreed to provide so many days' work on the farm. Although the cottier class was all but destroyed by the Famine, the concept survived and was applied to arrangements between farmers on the grounds that a conacre agreement did not interfere with the owner's rights. Farmers who owned some land that they were not in a position to cultivate that year, arranged with local auctioneers to let the conacre for the year. Although the term has been explained as an 'eleven month tenancy', it has no standing in law in Northern Ireland and is purely an arrangement. It is a useful device for farmers who wish to supplement grazing or take a cash crop, and essential for those who find that they can no longer work their land but are not in a position to sell it. Conacre land is the only land available for letting, and high rents have become customary because its price responds to general economic trends as well as changes in the circumstances of individual families. It is not too much to claim that conacre lubricates the operation of the land system throughout Ireland. Study of its operation in your townland over the past century should reveal much about the changes that have occurred in the management of land over the years.

All these factors, however, tended to confirm the strength of the relationship between farms and families. A survey of farming in the province as late as 1952 concluded: 'In Ulster the farm is usually a family concern and not only a livelihood but a way of life. Although the days of subsistence farming are gone, only the large farms are thought of as commercial enterprises'.[8] We can appreciate now that that great revolution has taken place during our own lifetime.

These changes in land ownership need to be viewed against the background of the great population changes that have swept over Ireland in the past three or four centuries. In Ulster the colonisation of both the hill country and the wastes of bogland was a consequence of the rapid increase in population. The consolidation of the family farm system has also to be seen against a long period of population decline that can best be studied in the census returns collected and prepared by the government.

The peak of the population explosion had been reached about the time of the 1841 census which was, by coincidence, the first census to provide population statistics by individual townlands rather than parishes. The territorial divisions used in the censuses of 1841 and 1851 were county, barony, parish, town and townland. From 1861 the parish was replaced by the Poor Law Union and Electoral Divisions. Nevertheless, the townland remained the basic unit until 1911 and was used also for the 1926 census in Northern Ireland. The figures were given under these headings:

Houses: inhabited, uninhabited, building, total
Persons: males, females, total

A table of these figures drawn from the censuses from 1841 to 1911 (or 1926) enables us to draw some conclusions about the rate of decline and its character. It is important to concentrate on the number of inhabited houses at each census rather than the total number, which includes both uninhabited houses and houses under construction. Any fall in the number of inhabited houses indicates the departure of whole families, no matter the size. When the number of persons drops without a corresponding drop in the number of houses, we may conclude that individuals were leaving home. The census abstracts indicate whether they were men or women.

The new valuation made by the government around 1860, along with its subsequent regular revisions, identifies the families that were leaving these houses so that we are given an opportunity to find out something more about them. Their names may appear in the records of the local churches and those of their children in the national school registers. We are fortunate that the actual census returns made by each household in Ireland are available for the 1901 and the 1911 censuses. They provide much useful information about religious affiliation, occupations, educational standards, counties of origin, and relationships within the families. Indeed, the older generation may be stimulated by a sight of the census returns to recall valuable information about some of the individuals mentioned.

This new valuation made by the government around 1860, with its revisions, also pinpoints the houses that were disappearing and records the approximate dates. The details illustrate the rapid decline of the characteristic cottier dwellings: many of them were pulled down while others were converted readily into out-buildings on farms. In the report of the 1841 census the government set out its method of classifying houses:

> The value or condition of a house, as to the accommodation it affords, may be considered to depend mainly on – 1st, its extent, as shown by the number of rooms; 2nd, its quality, as shown by the number of its windows; and 3rd, its solidity or durability, as shown by the material of its walls and roof. If numbers be adopted to express the position of every house in a scale of each of these elements, and if the numbers thus obtained for every house be added together, we shall have a new series of numbers, giving the position of the house in a scale compounded of all the elements. i.e. their actual state. We adopted four classes, and the result was, that in the lowest, or fourth class, were comprised all mud cabins having only one room; in the third, a better description of cottage, still built of mud, but varying from two to four rooms and windows; in the second a good farm-house, or in towns, a house in a small street, having from five to nine rooms and windows; and, in the first, all houses of a better description than the preceding classes.[9]

This programme appears to have continued without significant alteration. According to the actual census forms of the 1901 census, which are now held in the National Archives, Dublin, each enumerating constable was instructed to fill in the columns numbered 6 to 11 on the census form B1: House and Building Return:

6. WALLS: If walls are of stone, brick or concrete, enter the figure 1 in this column; if they are of mud, wood, or other perishable material, enter the figure 0.

7. ROOF: If roof is of slate, iron, or tiles, enter the figure 1 in this column; if it is of thatch, wood, or other perishable material, enter the figure 0.

8. ROOMS: Enter in this column:-

for each house with one room only the figure 1
for houses with 2, 3, or 4 rooms 2
"   5 or 6   "   3
"   7, 8 or 9   "   4
"   10, 11 or 12 "   5
"   13 or more "   6

9. WINDOWS IN FRONT: State in this column the exact number of windows in front of house.

10. TOT the figure you have entered in columns 6, 7, 8 and 9, and enter the total for each house in this column.

11. CLASS OF HOUSE: When total in column 10 is

1 or 2   enter   '4th'
3, 4 or 5   "   '3rd'
6, 7, 8, 9, 10 or 11   "   '2nd'
12 or over   "   '1st'[10]

Unfortunately, such a classification system conceals the major factor of the durability of the houses according to the materials used in their construction. We should classify them instead according to the information in columns 6 and 7: (i) mud and thatch; (ii) mud and permanent roof [slate, iron, or tiles]; (iii) brick or stone [or concrete] and thatch; (iv) brick or stone [or concrete] and permanent roof. This enables us to distinguish the vernacular houses defined in the first three classes from the new labourers' cottages and the 'improved' houses being built by the farmers. Large numbers of labourers cottages were built by the new Rural District Councils (created by the Local Government Act of 1898) to carry out the terms of the Labourers (Ireland) Acts of 1883 and 1906. Information about their construction can be found in the records of the rural district councils. They were built by local contractors using the same kinds of materials and techniques that they used in the new two-storey houses for the wealthier farmers. These substantial farmhouses attracted special attention in the notebooks made by the valuators engaged on the annual revision (PRONI, VAL 12E and the Valuation Office in Dublin).

III

It has to be remembered that little of the land in Ulster is naturally fertile, and that most of the good land is to be found in river valleys. Much of the remainder of the province is occupied by mountains covered with blanket bog. At the time of the Plantation, bog covered many square miles of the lowlands also. Immigrants from Britain then initiated drainage projects in districts such as north Armagh. In the barony of Oneilland, for example, the Civil Survey of the mid-1650s recorded:

> The soil of this barony is generally good for tillage and pasture and the finest plantation of Ulster by reason of the English nation that first planted it, most of the same being naturally subject to wet but by their industry drained and made dry.[11]

However, attempts by the planters to improve poor soils by adding natural fertilisers such as lime and sand often failed because the annual rainfall was considerable enough to leach the soils, especially in the north and west of the province. The eighteenth century, however, witnessed an increasing optimism about the efficacy of new techniques in the improvement of marginal land. When bog was well-trenched with the spade it dried out and could then be cultivated with potatoes that in their turn cleared the ground of weeds and made it fit to bear crops of oats. On such land a long, heavy spade, termed in Irish the 'loy', was used to undercut sods and then lever them over to form lazy-beds which were preferred to drills for cultivation by the small-farmers. Although the extent of cultivation was always limited by the amount of manure that a farm could produce, farmers became very skilful at eking it out by composting it with loam or ashes. In order to save the grain in the head, corn crops were harvested with the sickle while grass was mowed with the scythe. It was not until after the Famine that corn began to be cut by the scythe and soon afterwards the horse-drawn reaper was introduced.

The first two years of the Famine forced the government to recognise the need for an accurate estimate of agricultural output throughout Ireland. From 1847, therefore, figures for both crop acreage and domestic animals were collected by the constabulary. The whole project was based on the unit of the townland and twenty-four questions had to be answered about each of some 60,760 townlands. These townlands were grouped into their Poor Law Unions and for the first few years only, ending in 1851, detailed information was provided for each of the Electoral Divisions into which each Union could be subdivided. As a result, it is possible to obtain a valuable snapshot of agriculture in your district by examining the acreage of the various crops grown in the Electoral District that contains your townland. After 1851 a Poor Law Boundary Commission redrew the Electoral Districts.

Although the compilers relied on the constabulary to provide them with the 'extent of land under crops', they also employed local people with farming experience each autumn to estimate the 'quantity of produce for each district' and, later, to report on the quality of the crops harvested. Because the bulk of the crops was used to feed animals, the government decided also to count livestock: these figures were totalled by counties and subdivided into baronies. Their concern to relate changes in the number of livestock to the 'class of persons' that kept the animals, led them to introduce a scale of 'sizes of holdings' : (a) less than one acre, (b) 1 – 5 acres, (c) 5 – 15 acres, (d) 15 – 30 acres, and (e) over 30 acres. This idea was extended to the acreage under crops. As a result, the tables became too specialised to shed light on the changes at townland or even electoral division level: the poor law union became the unit. After 1874 even the farm-size breakdown was abandoned.

Nevertheless, all these details were published annually in the parliamentary papers and much can be learned from studying the trends. The figures show that the overall crop area continued to increase up to 1860, which was the peak year in the late nineteenth century. Oats then occupied almost half the total crop land, but after 1860 their share declined to about one quarter by 1900 with the spread of grassland: wheat and barley acreages soon became insignificant. The potato crop recovered quickly after 1848 to produce excellent crops throughout the 1850s. After 1860, however, the acreage under potatoes gradually fell in proportion to the decline in population: most of the crop was consumed on the farms by humans and animals. As blight remained a problem, some farmers preferred to cultivate swede turnips which were reckoned to yield as much milk and manure as the same quantity of potatoes. Not until the late 1890s did the practice of spraying the tops of the potato plants with Bordeaux mixture each summer become widespread.

The major cash crop was flax to supply the linen industry but, after the great expansion of that industry to take advantage of the cotton famine occasioned by the American Civil War in the early 1860s, the acreage under flax declined steadily. Its yields and prices could not compete with pastoral farming nor, especially after 1890, with the grass seed trade which fitted better into the new crop rotations, stimulated as they were by the use of artificial fertilisers such as superphosphate and sulphate of ammonia.

The introduction and spread of the use of artificial fertilisers, along with the rapid growth of the agricultural engineering industry, has given the term 'the second agricultural revolution' to the period 1820-80 throughout the British Isles. We should consider the impact of these changes on our townland. The introduction of mineral fertilisers and of specific kinds of machinery can tell us something about the prosperity of individual farms or groups of farmers. Details about those among them who participated in agricultural shows can be found in local newspapers. Farmers required capital and knowledge to make such investments. They needed security in their own holdings as well as the opportunity to acquire more land. Where they had such support, a class of strong farmers emerged, bought out their smaller neighbours, and engaged in commercial farming. However, in those regions divided into tiny farms, such as south Ulster, this process of consolidation took much longer. The family farm had labour to spare and the traditional hand implements could cope with all the jobs around the farm. Hired help was cheap and readily available. It was only the more ambitious and well-doing farmers who purchased reapers, barn threshers and churns.

AGRICULTURAL MACHINES IN IRELAND 1865–1895[12]

	1865	1875	1881	1886	1890	1895
Churning Machines	848	2,953	2,856	2,653	2,796	3,241
Grubbers	812	741	565	225	302	465
Hay, Chaff & Straw Cutters	1,208	1,425	2,124	254	305	376
Hay Rakes	2,478	5,618	4,420	3,525	4,121	7,184
Mowing & Reaping Machines	1,085	10,016	11,708	9,014	11,505	14,704
Potato Diggers	10	15	38	175	228	477
Threshing Machines	9,180	12,410	13,295	7,043	7,894	8,546
Turnip Slicers	792	1,621	1,491	593	570	819

The revolution in farming, as it worked out on the ground, is well summed up in this undated and unsigned memorandum, found loose in a rental in Lord Lurgan's estate office:

> It is not by selling crops in the market that many of the farmers live. It is by rearing and feeding cattle, horses, pigs on the farm produce. Calves of a year and a quarter old are frequently sold at £10; forty years ago, the best cow brought into market would not have given much more. Pork at the above date frequently sold at £1.16s. per cwt., now it is sold at £2.16s. per cwt. Grass seed till of late years was thrown into the dunghill, it is now sold at £1 per cwt. and many take off as much grass seed as pays their rents. Beef at the above date, nearly best in market was bought at 4d per lb, now from 10d to 1s.per lb. Butter at above date, best in maket sold from 6d to 8d per

lb., now from 1s to 1s.6d per lb. Eggs formerly sold at 4d per dozen, now from 1s. to 1s.4d. Rents with many were as high then as now. Labouring men's pay as a rule in country places is not more than 2d to 4d per day of a rise. Some of your tenants on Richmount estate notwithstanding having paid hundreds of pounds of bail money for their friends were able to buy farm after farm all taken off the land they now say is ruining them.[13]

IV

Since the Plantation, Ulster has been well served by numerous market towns and the density of its road network in some places is among the highest in western Europe. That character has owed much to the compact estates granted by the crown to the new landlords, for it was they who encouraged the creation of numerous market towns linked to each other by tracks. Under an act of 1615, responsibility for the construction and maintenance of these roads had been imposed on each parish by requiring it to organise its inhabitants to provide six days' free labour on the roads each year. Only the building of bridges was made the responsibility of the justices of the peace for each county, and they were enabled to levy a county tax or cess with the assent of the grand jury. In these circumstances the quality of local roads depended on the initiative of the landlord or his agent.

By the early eighteenth century the parish system could not cope with the increase of road traffic generated by the growing domestic linen industry. The first government solution was the introduction of turnpike roads in the 1730s in the east of the province, but they were not extensive enough to cope with the demand. In 1758 parliament decided to exempt day labourers from the statutory six days' labour because compulsory unpaid work was recognised as 'burthensome to the poor', a move that threw the burden of statutory labour back on to the small farmers, cottiers, and weavers. As a result of the Oakboy disturbances that followed, parliament passed the 1765 Road Act to abolish the six days labour and to authorise the grand jury of each county to raise a county tax or cess, to build and maintain roads and bridges.

This act changed the national attitude to road-building. More and more money became available for the renewal of the road network and it was seen as an ideal way to employ the labourers. Within the following century, thousands of miles were constructed or remodelled throughout Ireland, and they opened up many square miles of marginal land to colonisation and cultivation. This revolution can best be traced on the large wall maps of individual counties, prepared for their respective grand juries and hung in the courthouses for regular consultation. Most valuable in this context is John Lendrick's map of county Antrim of 1780 which was updated in 1808 to incorporate the revised network of roads: comparison of the two maps reveals the vast increase not only in the mileage of roads, but in the great stretches of countryside that were made accessible. John McEvoy, in his *Statistical survey of the county of Tyrone* (1802), confirmed these observations for his own county when he recommended the updating of the county map made for the grand jury by the McCrea brothers between 1774 and 1776.

Landlords were not slow to take advantage of this unique opportunity to obtain tenants. Many of them promoted or revived market-towns on their estates because the law stipulated that main roads could be laid out only between market-towns or (after 1765) between market-towns and the seacoast.[14] The landlords often indicated their intention by paying the crown to grant them patents permitting them to hold weekly markets in their towns. They were then in a position to apply to the grand jury to link every new town with its neighbours, and this process extended the network of roads throughout the countryside. Of course, in the long run many of these new market-towns failed to develop or sustain a weekly market, but the new roads continued to be maintained at the charge of the county.

These new roads also opened up the country for settlement and facilitated the transport of turf, timber, lime, and manure as well as provisions and animals to market. Soon there was a great increase in the number of wheel-cars kept by farmers and after 1800 the Scotch cart, drawn by heavy horses, became a more familiar sight throughout the province. Along the new roads landlords marked out farms, often providing timber and lime for the new tenants to build houses. By charging low rents the landlords were able to attract many families who could not compete in the well-populated lowlands. It was the newcomers who created farms for succeeding generations of their families. The colonisation of the uplands, bogs and other waste lands during the century before the Famine is one of the most underrated factors in the making of the Irish landscape. The hill people were serviced by the small market-towns with their hardware stores, local craftsmen, and monthly fair-days, so that the government valuers took into account the distance of each farm from the neighbouring towns.

It is important, therefore, to examine first the Ordnance Survey maps and then the county maps as well as estate maps to determine what impact the construction of new roads had on your townland. The First Valuation may be especially valuable in considering these questions. Did any of these roads cut through or modify older field boundaries, as the railway was often to do in the 1840s? Did it lead to the dispersal of farm-houses throughout the townland, the construction of new houses (often along the new road), or the reorientation of existing houses with their rights-of-way? Did it open up access to new quarries, limepits, and turf-banks? Did it affect the way its inhabitants viewed neighbouring towns and townlands?

The great importance of the road network in Ulster was eclipsed in men's minds for nearly a century by the advent of the railways in the 1830s. Most of the carriage of goods and passengers was transferred from the cart and the stage-coach on the roads to the new lines of railway track that searched out the easiest gradients from one river valley to the next. Instead, the local railway station became an institution and a focus for both economic and social activity as speeds rose and charges fell. Towns without stations were bypassed and lost their fairs and markets to better-placed rivals. By the 1930s, however, with the development of the petrol engine, road transport was coming back. It provided dealers with their own transport, enabling them to visit the farms and purchase on the doorstep, especially eggs and potatoes. Delivery men too graduated from horse-transport to motor-transport. The second half of the twentieth century has witnessed a revolution in road-transport, with container-lorries penetrating into every farmyard.

V

In the final instance it has to be reiterated that at the heart of all this research lies the history of a community. We should consider first the origins of this community in the period under review. Was this townland occupied by British settlers or did it remain in the possession of native families? The history of several townlands suggests that throughout the seventeenth century British immigrants continued to secure leases at the expense of native families, but that quite early in the eighteenth century some kind of balance was struck, in spite of the Penal Laws. After that time the character of a townland was less likely to change its ethnic complexion. Even if the lease of the townland was in the hands of a Protestant middleman the Catholic undertenants would often be left to organise the pattern of landholding among themselves: in time they would gain recognition as tenants of their farms. It is important to identify such groups within each townland and especially their leaders. They often played a leading role also in the congregations of local churches and the management of national schools, and in return they looked to the clergy and the schoolmaster for active support.

Another major factor in the every-day life of the community was the presence or absence of a landlord or his resident agent. The community would benefit if there was someone there to manage the estate, provide leadership and employment, and sort out problems and quarrels. Without him, problems would undermine community spirit and bad blood run from generation to generation. A well-managed estate attracted tenants, and most of the serious problems were created by tenants rather than by their landlord. Relations between landlords and tenants did deteriorate by the mid nineteenth century due to changing circumstances, and culminated by the end of the century in the sale of many estates to the tenants. Although tenant ownership gave the farmer security before the law, it did not bring prosperity in the long agricultural slump that lasted from the 1880s to the 1930s.

In the hope that competition among buyers would mean better prices for their crops and stock, farmers attended weekly markets and the seasonal or monthly 'fair-days' in all the neighbouring towns. Although the townspeople resented the mess and inconvenience caused on these occasions, they needed the custom of the farmers. While they were there they frequented shops, forges (and later, garages), tradesmen, pubs and solicitors' offices and were likely to run up considerable debts. In turn, their farms were visited by pedlars, cattle dealers, egg and poultry men, bread and grocery salesmen, and an increasing number of government officials.

That heyday has gone. Over the past century and a half the population of many townlands has been decimated and rural community life continues to decline with the advance of commercial agriculture. Soon it may be too late to research their history.

1. J. Mallory, T. McNeill, *The archaeology of Ulster* (Belfast, 1991).
2. Katharine Simms, *From kings to warlords* (Woodbridge, 1987).
3. J. H. Andrews, 'The maps of the escheated counties of Ulster 1609-10' in *Proceedings of the Royal Irish Academy*, lxxiv, section C, no 4. (1974).
4. *Calendar of State Papers, Ireland, 1625-32*, pp. 349-52.
5. W. H. Crawford, 'The significance of landed estates in Ulster, 1600-1820' in *Irish Economic and Social History*, xvii (1990), pp. 53-5.
6. Griffith's Valuation c.1860 (Public Record Office of Northern Ireland VAL 2B).
7. W. E. Vaughan, *Landlords and tenants in mid-Victorian Ireland* (Oxford, 1994), p. 39.
8. D. A. Hill, 'Land use' in Emrys Jones (ed.), *Belfast in its regional setting* (Belfast, 1952), p. 166.
9. *Report of the commissioners appointed to take the census of Ireland for the year 1841* [504], H. C. 1843, xxiv, 14.
10. *Report of the commissioners appointed to take the census of Ireland for the year 1841* [504], H. C. 1843, xxiv, 14.
11. R. Simington (ed.), *The civil survey A.D. 1654-1656*, (10 vols. Dublin, 1931-61) x, p. 69.
12. Information extracted from Table 19 'Agricultural machines' in *Agricultural statistics for the year 1895* [G -8126] H.C. 1896, xcii, 388.
13. Quoted in F. X McCorry, *Lurgan: an Irish provincial town, 1610- 1970* (Lurgan, 1993), p. 93.
14. 5 Geo. III, c.14, s.6.

THE BUILT HERITAGE AND
THE LOCAL HISTORIAN

Nick Brannon

The local historian searching for subject material needs only to look around. Little of the appearance of the Irish landscape is 'natural'. Fields, buildings, settlements, boundaries, place-names, roads, railways and canals, fill our maps. They reflect thousands of years of agriculture, industry, construction, settlement and communications. There is no cut-off date for studies of the built heritage; techniques of recording, description and interpretation may be applied to the debris left by prehistoric hunter-gatherers, to medieval church ruins or to a census of twentieth-century military installations.

The gathering of information on the built heritage (a collective term now embracing archaeological sites and monuments, historic buildings, gardens and estates, industrial and maritime archaeology, with archaeological excavation and the archaeological objects recovered from them) became a function of the Northern Ireland government in 1950, when the Archaeological Survey was set up in the Ministry of Finance. The role of 'the Survey', as it came to be known, was to be similar to that of the Royal Commissions on Ancient and Historical Monuments established in England, Scotland and Wales in 1908 – that of archaeological and architectural recording. The Commissions, however, have recently celebrated the fiftieth anniversaries of their National Monuments Records, established at the end of World War II in the recognition that heritage (particularly historic buildings) was being lost without record. The National Monuments Records have always had a public access function, but until 1992 there was no such formal access to information gathered in Northern Ireland.

The Archaeological Survey was initially staffed by just two archaeologists, Dudley Waterman and Pat Collins. Much of their work (and that of their successors) can be seen in the annual *Ulster Journal of Archaeology*[1] from the 1950s, and in *An Archaeological Survey of County Down* (1966)[2]. Their archaeological survey and excavations, and their architectural recording, is built on information gathered by cartographers, local historians and antiquarians, amateur and university archaeologists and historical geographers from the nineteenth century onwards. Their standards set a level which their successors have striven to maintain.

Professional staffing grew gradually, but 'the Survey' is no more, its professional identity and data holdings now lying within the Built Heritage directorate of the Environment and Heritage Service (EHS), an agency within the Department of the Environment for Northern Ireland (DoENI). The directorate is staffed by ten archaeologists and six architects (with conservation, photographic and drafting specialists and administrative and contracted support) whose duties span survey, research, excavation, conservation, statutory protection, and promotion of the built heritage through publication, education and public relations.

Built heritage information held by EHS is freely available, subject to certain reasonable conditions, under the Environmental Information Regulations (NI) 1993, which stem from a European Community directive. The protection of the built heritage is an environmental issue – the destruction of ancient sites, or historic monuments and buildings must be an environmental concern. Such sites can only rarely be 'sustainably' developed. Once destroyed, they are gone for ever. The local historian, within this thinking, is a *de facto* environmentalist who can help to police the landscape with an historical perspective. Built heritage data, then, may be the only records that survive to attest to the former existence of a monument or building. The records held by EHS can be accessed through the Monuments and Buildings Record (MBR), the public access facility housed in the EHS offices in Hill Street, on the edge of Belfast city centre.

The MBR was officially opened by Robert Atkins, then Minister for the Environment, on 27 October 1992, fulfilling a commitment made by his predecessor Peter Bottomley two years earlier, and a government White Paper undertaking. Internally, the MBR is an everyday working tool, but it is in its public access role that it has a growing identity and outreach. The MBR is the sum of its parts, the collective name for numerous databases, archives and collections. It is not a static archive, but rather an evolving resource. Information is continually being gathered, analysed and catalogued. Donations and archive acquisitions add to collections.

The MBR's holdings have value as (priceless) archive documents, as (oftentimes unique) records, and as a concentrated source of information. Some local historians have already identified the MBR as a valuable resource, while others remain to be made aware of its riches and potential. At the time of writing the MBR provides access to built heritage information through meeting some 1,300 telephoned, written and in-person inquiries per year. Private research (which includes local historians) accounts for 50 per cent of the inquiries, with another 40 per cent meeting education curriculum resource needs. Tourism, commercial and environmental assessment inquiries comprise the remainder.

Several particular projects and stand-alone archives, built up over many years, are the foundation stones which support the MBR. Longest established and most developed is the Sites and Monuments Record (SMR), a basic record of the approximately 14,600 archaeological sites and monuments currently identified in the province (all figures are approximate, rounded up to the nearest hundred). From the early 1970s, when archaeologists began to assemble the SMR, every archaeological site and monument (whether or not visible on today's landscape) has been uniquely identified on a map.

In the early 1980s copies of SMR maps and checklists were widely distributed to land-using agencies – planning, agriculture, forestry, drainage for instance – to provide an early warning system for consultation should sites be threatened with damage or destruction by development or land-use proposals. From 1985 to 1994 the number of planning consultations affecting historic monuments rose from 191 to 448, and this year will exceed 500. Copies of local SMR maps have also been provided to some local history societies.

The unique identifying numbers (relating to county, Ordnance Survey six inch to the mile map sheet number, and a unique number within the area covered by the map) are the link to card indices, site description files, excavation archives and archaeological objects, published and unpublished references, photographs, slides and measured drawings, reflecting over 8,000 years of human impact on the landscape, from the Mesolithic (Middle Stone Age) period to post-medieval times.

A 1996 analysis of data held in the SMR identified 5,000 archaeological sites and monuments in county Antrim and 2,800 in county Down, reflecting the size of the counties, their high quality agricultural land and the maritime trading and exploitation advantages gained from the Irish Sea. County Tyrone, with 2,000 sites, is also relatively large, with several distinct regions. The lower number of sites reflects its largely upland topography, which, although attractive for prehistoric peoples before the onset of concealing blanket peat, was thereafter relatively under-occupied during the Early Christian and medieval periods. Together with county Londonderry, with 1,900 sites, these two counties have the greatest potential for new discoveries, with ongoing bog surveys revealing 'hidden' sites. Counties Armagh and

Aerial photograph of Rathtrillick Rath, Co. Armagh showing a landscape influenced by man over the centuries. DOENI photograph 15:20/3, 1977.

Fermanagh, with 1,000 and 1,900 sites respectively, are the most-studied counties. Publication of inventories of their sites and monuments is expected within a few years.

A numerical breakdown by chronological period and conventional monument types throughout Northern Ireland reveals that Early Christian period sites are by far the most numerous, with some 5,000 raths (called 'enclosures' where their accurate dating and identification is indeterminate, and might only be confirmed by excavation). Ecclesiastical sites (whether churches, crosses, holy wells, bullauns or monastic enclosures) form the second largest group. Third come secular monuments (other than raths) – souterrains, crannogs, cashels and mounds, although some of these latter may be prehistoric or medieval. The prehistoric monuments follow, with individual standing stones, megalithic tombs, cairns and stone circles. Medieval castles and Plantation bawns with associated villages bring up the rear. Over fifty towns and villages in Northern Ireland are recognised as having historic origins which may yield archaeological data, and where the alert local historian can contribute through the surveillance of foundation or service trenches and the reporting of any observations.

Most of these sites are, or have been (within the last 150 years) visible in the landscape as upstanding earthworks, megaliths or buildings. Many are marked on Ordnance Survey maps. Sample calculations of survival rates in the late 1970s, based on map attributions, suggest that up to 50 per cent of sites (particularly earthworks) have been destroyed as landscape features in south county Antrim and county Armagh, with 10 per cent of known sites lost in county Fermanagh.

The absence of a site as a visible landscape feature does not necessarily mean that archaeology underground is also absent. Where no upstanding traces remain, aerial photography can detect buried archaeological remains by the effect that they have on the growth of crops. Recent work by Queen's University archaeologists at the Giant's Ring, a large circular earthwork outside Belfast, has revealed an extensive prehistoric ritual complex on the evidence of superb aerial photographic evidence, and much of this evidence has been confirmed by excavation. The surveillance of the natural gas pipeline installation on Islandmagee (effectively a random slice through the landscape) has revealed the remains of two neolithic houses whose presence was otherwise unknown and unpredictable. Self-evidently, many sites yet remain to be discovered throughout the Northern Ireland landscape.

Similarly, map-based systems and unique identifiers locate and identify sites within the parallel collections, described below. Built heritage information is mostly recorded using *pro formas* which meet European 'core data' standards, including mandatory locational and descriptive data suitable for computerised interrogation. For the local historian interested in the archaeological landscape, this is a definitive resource.

For schools or local history groups, one of the best long-term investments that generations of pupils or members can make in the future is to establish a local sites and monument record with systematised gathering of the archaeological data in their catchment area. This could expand into records of historic buildings, industrial archaeology or other areas, described below. While detailed surveying and measured recording require specialist knowledge and vocabulary, many local historians have made important contributions and there are good examples in society and local history journals. The great advantage that local historians enjoy over the (often Belfast-based) 'professional' is that they *are* local, and can cross physical and cultural boundaries which may be obstacles to 'the man from the Ministry'.

Photographic records of landscapes, streetscapes and settings, the chronological and genealogical mapping of graveyards (with tombstone typology) or farming taboos (against damaging historic sites, cutting down a fairy thorn, or opening a souterrain) can be mapped. A local history lecture, a visit to make a survey, home-school links, or a piece in the local press, can stimulate instant recall from an owner, a polished stone axe from a mantel-piece, a local place-name, the memory of 'bones'. The SMR is a model for data capture and storage. One of the most significant contributions that any local historian can make is to ensure that his or her information can be accessed by, and shared with, others.

In earlier decades, when protection measures were less effective than they are today, the response to threats to archaeological sites was usually through rescue excavation. Sometimes known in archaeologists' jargon as 'mitigation by record', excavation embraces the paradox that the archaeologist destroys the resource being excavated. Archaeological deposits can only be excavated once, hence the painstaking techniques employed. Though the rescue 'agenda' is necessarily dictated by threats rather than research criteria, results have been fruitful, and can be seen particularly in reports in the annual *Ulster Journal of Archaeology*, or *Pieces of the Past*[3] which highlights the results of thirty-five rescue excavations carried out between 1970 (the beginning of the rescue 'boom') and 1986.

While many long-established historical societies in England have a record of archaeological excavation and field-walking, such amateur work is rarely seen in Northern Ireland. The statutory licensing of excavations (currently under provisions of the Historic Monuments and Archaeological Objects (NI) Order 1995, but in force under earlier legislation since 1937), health and safety and insurance requirements, and the sheer pace required in a rescue excavation context have, no doubt, been disincentives against amateur involvement.

In the last few years policies and practice have been developed towards the protection of sites, monuments and their settings, and the Department of the Environment's *Planning Strategy for Rural Northern Ireland* (1993)[4] estab-lished important best practice for archaeological conservation, placing the onus on developers to anticipate, avoid where possible, and mitigate threats to the heritage. The rescue boom appears to be over, and its excavation work-load is anyway largely in the hands of private sector contract archaeologists working within archaeological planning conditions. Any local historian seek-ing excavation experience is more likely to find it through participation as a volunteer in occasional university research excavations. Some local historical societies have carried out artefact-search fieldwalking in ploughland, under professional supervision. Fieldwalking can be labour intensive, and training is required, but such participation can be rewarding.

The recording of historic buildings was part of the Archaeological Survey function from the 1950s onwards, but much of this work was sampling or reactive and carried no statutory implications. Since the passing of planning legislation which introduced the 'listing' of buildings of historic or architectural interest in 1972, the Department of the Environment has statutorily protected some 8,500 historic buildings in Northern Ireland. Summary details of these listed buildings are available for public consultation in the MBR. Over 40,000 colour transparencies and 40,000 black-and-white photographs of historic buildings (both listed and unlisted) are held by EHS, but not all are sufficiently catalogued to be readily accessible to the public. Cataloguing of photographs, drawings and other documents is a constant workload within the MBR. The Irish Architectural Archive in Dublin has a volunteer support group and it is one of the aims of the MBR to encourage individuals to contribute to this work.

A second, systematic 'listing' survey of the historic buildings of the province is now underway. Thematic work, such as the Buildings at Risk project carried out by the Ulster Architectural Heritage Society with EHS support, and a survey of thatched buildings, is ongoing. Threats to buildings still prompt recording surveys. The evidence that McHugh's Bar, near the Albert Clock in Belfast city centre, is Belfast's oldest (known) surviving building,

The reconstructed 1674 Coleraine town house at the Ulster Folk and Transport Museum. DOENI photograph L'D 72/13, 1991.

was revealed during such a reactive survey. One of the most remarkable architectural discoveries in recent times has been the discovery of the later-sixteenth-century Newry Castle, long thought to be lost but revealed as still standing to its original three storeys, within the fabric of a later building. Such discoveries (as with Ulster's oldest surviving townhouse in Coleraine, built in New Row in 1674 and now restored for display in the Ulster Folk and Transport Museum) demonstrate that familiar urban streets may contain 'lost' historic buildings, hidden by later rendering or pierced by later openings, but recoverable through property research and acute or chance observation. In the countryside too, older houses are often replaced rather than demolished, and may be reused for non-domestic purposes. Some buildings of clay or mud still survive. How many there are, where they are, and what histories they hold, is another challenge.

The three-year Northern Ireland Building Record Project, set up at the Queen's University Institute of Irish Studies in 1985, and supported by the Department of the Environment, was a feasibility study to research sources of records and systems to manage them. Three junior fellows of the Institute examined the workings of the National Monuments Records in Edinburgh and London, and the Irish Architectural Archive in Dublin, and catalogued over 4,000 architectural archive accessions (maps, architectural drawings and photographs) made during the Project. Their research established that there was a clear public and professional demand for a publicly-accessible resource, which was realised with the opening of the MBR in 1992. The opening was preceded, by a few days, by the acquisition through purchase of the Clokey Stained Glass Collection. The Clokey Studios, employing up to fifty staff in the Smithfield area of Belfast, was destroyed by fire in the 1970s, when all records and stained-glass designs housed there were lost. Fortunately, some of original designs had been stored elsewhere, and 180 of them (including domestic, symbolic, figurative, heraldic and memorial glass, drawn in inks and water colours, or pastel crayon) were put up for sale by Harold Clokey, son of the founder of the firm. The designs date from the 1920s onwards, and a three-volume typological catalogue of the MBR holdings has been produced. Clokey's original working catalogue, which recorded whether the designs were ever manufactured and where they were installed, had been destroyed in the fire. While a few of the designs carry inscriptions recording their destination (one window was intended for a church in Ghana), most cannot be correlated with *in situ* church or civic windows, and this remains a challenge for the enthusiast.

Several valuable architectural archive collections, acquired over many years but virtually inaccessible until MBR space and resources became available, can now be consulted. Some 12,000 working drawings by architects John MacGeagh and Robert McKinstry have been individually identified, with 385 boxes of associated documents. The Public Record Office of Northern Ireland has loaned the John Seeds photographic collection, mostly of Georgian architecture. Works Service files held by the Public Record Office of Northern Ireland and destined for disposal were culled and yielded a small archive of drawings and photographs of public buildings, schools and institutions. More recently, over 3,000 photographs, reflecting James Stevens Curl's 1965-91 researches on Northern Ireland buildings, have been acquired through purchase, while others (including chance passers-by) have donated personal collections. These collections contain a wealth of information which will reward detailed research.

Pioneering work on the industrial heritage paralleled archaeological survey in the 1950s, and saw fruit in E. R. R. Green's *The industrial archaeology of county Down* (1963)[5] From this sprang Alan McCutcheon's *The industrial archaeology of Northern Ireland* (1980).[6] McCutcheon's survey generated a large archive, including 20,000 black-and-white photographs, first housed in the Public Record Office of Northern Ireland, but later transferred to the MBR stores as a more appropriate repository. Several years' work remain to fully assimilate the archive into the MBR for easy public access; research work which would be appropriate in an MBR 'friends' or volunteer programme.

From 1982 to 1985, the Industrial Archaeology Record (IAR), later renamed the Industrial Heritage Record (IHR) was compiled through the Department of Environment-funded tenure of a fellowship at the Queen's University Institute of Irish Studies. As with the early stages of the SMR, the IHR was largely a map-based, 'paper' survey which identified some 15,000 sites. The IHR did not include Belfast, but this shortfall was made good in 1987-88 when, in connection with the Belfast Urban Area Plan, the Department of Environment funded contract staff to compile an industrial heritage record for Greater Belfast. The Greater Belfast Industrial Archaeological Survey (GBIAS) identified 1,100 sites from map sources and included some photographic fieldwork. The recording programme for the next three years proposes detailed, high-level surveying of some 600 industrial monuments throughout the province and a largely desk-based, 'paper' survey of Northern Ireland lighthouses and associated features. Industrial archaeology has few 'professional' practitioners in Ireland, and it has always (in its short history) benefited from local enthusiasm and hands-on commitment. Many themes and places would benefit from detailed research. For example, local lime-kilns dot the maps of rural Northern Ireland, and a map and fieldwork recording census of these kilns, with local historical research behind it, is a prime candidate for the support of local studies groups.

In 1989 the Northern Ireland Heritage Gardens Committee raised funds, again including monies from Department of Environment, to support an Institute of Irish Studies Fellow in building up a record of Northern Ireland gardens. Over three years archival research was combined with fieldwork and in 1992 the Heritage Gardens Inventory, detailing 648 sites, was issued. The inventory was lodged with the MBR, since when further work has been completed to link entries for the gardens with archaeological and architectural sites located in their environs. The follow-up stage is the production of a Gardens Register, reflecting quality criteria, as a tool to aid the protection of historic gardens through planning and advisory processes. Historic gardens are not static entities – their landscapes remain while their flora is renewed, though their settings may change – but they remain places of special historic interest, offering a unique blend of 'built' and 'natural' heritage research.

Recent years have seen a growing awareness of the importance of the maritime heritage. Over the last three years EHS has funded a fellowship at the Institute of Irish Studies towards the creation of a Maritime Record. Documentary information on some 3,000 shipwrecks in Northern Ireland waters, reflecting eighteenth- to twentieth-century records, has been assembled. Information on net-snags and other sea-bed features, supplied by the fishing community, suggests that several thousand other wrecks remain to be identified, although there are practical problems in matching documentary accounts with sea-bed locations: the process known as 'ground truthing'.

A recent successful venture involved the statutorily-licensed archaeological investigation of the wreck of the *Taymouth Castle*, which sank off the county Antrim coast in 1868, *en route* from Scotland to Singapore. Shipping records provide considerable detail about its cargo. Hundreds of fragments of Glasgow 'sponge-ware' pottery were recovered from the cargo mound on the sea bed, along with intact, corked glass bottles. While the bottled contents remained alcoholic, the liquor was not potable. Inclination and training (including stringent health and safety demands) limit opportunities for the average terrestrial archaeologist as well as the average local historian. The sports-diving community includes those who shared their identification of the *Taymouth Castle* wreck with the public, thus ensuring its archaeological investigation (and the return of the artefacts to curation in a Glasgow museum). Local historians preferring to keep their feet dry can set these wrecks in a shipping, fishing, trade and emigration context.

A new fieldwork undertaking is generating fascinating information. Examination of the inter-tidal zone (that area of land covered at high tide and exposed at low tide, otherwise known as the foreshore) ringing Strangford Lough has revealed man-made features including fish-traps, kelp farms, jetties, slipways, artificial shellfish beds and flint tools, found within submerged Mesolithic woodland. Again, such fieldwork requires training, particularly in health and safety, and should not be undertaken without risk assessment. Mapping in such a physically blank landscape (hundreds of metres from the shore yet less than a wellington boot deep in water) can also pose problems. As a new form of landscape survey it perfectly illustrates the value of 'getting one's eye in'. One must also learn to relate foreshore exploitation to the dry land landscape history which borders it.

The most 'recent' archaeological landscape is that encompassed by Northern Ireland's participation in the Defence of Britain Project, which aims to document (from readily-accessible public sources) and survey, in the field, the military fortifications, buildings and installations which survive from the World Wars. As in the various spheres of archaeology, architecture, industry, gardens and maritime archaeology, there are numerous non-salaried enthusiasts who already contribute their time and skills in gathering data on twentieth-century military history and its physical remains. 1997 saw the 'recruitment' of thirty volunteers towards a comprehensive survey undertaken with uniform recording standards. The record will be housed in the MBR.

Donations and contacts continue to be made. A dozen privately-owned Clokey stained-glass window designs were recently brought in for examination and photographic copying. A passing member of the McCausland family was delighted to see an MBR window display including detailed drawings of the McCausland building in Belfast, produced as part of the architectural recording programme, and brought in an early twentieth-century photograph of the building to add to the archive. An outreach project, aimed particularly at individuals and businesses holding architectural archives is underway. No doubt there are many unique built heritage records which would be saved from decay or destruction if their owners were aware that a home could be found for them in the MBR, thus preserving them for posterity, and donations will always be welcome. The Monuments and Buildings Record will always be an evolving resource, a repository for records of monuments and buildings freely available to anyone, particularly the local historian, who cares to consult and contribute towards it.

1. Ulster Archaeological Society, *Ulster journal of archaeology* (3rd series) (Belfast).
2. E. M. Jope (ed.), *An archaeological survey of county Down* (HMSO, Belfast, 1966).
3. Ann Hamlin and C. J. Lynn (eds), *Pieces of the past* (HMSO, Belfast, 1988).
4. Department of the Environment, *A planning strategy for rural Northern Ireland* (HMSO, Belfast, 1993).
5. E. R. R. Green *The industrial archaeology of county Down* (HMSO, Belfast, 1963).
6. W. A. McCutcheon, *The industrial archaeology of Northern Ireland* (HMSO, Belfast, 1980).

The Monuments and Buildings Record is housed in the Environment and Heritage Service premises at 5-33 Hill Street, near Belfast city centre. It is open on weekdays, except public holidays, between 9.30am – 4.30pm, though closed at lunchtime between 1pm – 2pm. Telephone enquiries may be made to (01232) 235000, facsimile enquiries to (01232) 543111.

THE COMPARATIVE ASPECT IN LOCAL STUDIES

John Lynch

The study of a locality or a community is a valid form of historical research and one which frequently adds useful specific information to broader accounts. However, there is an inherent danger that such studies can not only be distinctive from broader history but also separate from it. There may be tendency for research projects to become 'parochial' rather than 'local'. This is understandable; the researcher becomes engrossed in the detail of the project, which may have personal or family interest, and begins to consider everything else as irrelevant. The result can be highly detailed, carefully researched, well written but limited.

Communities and geographic areas do not exist in isolation; like people they are the product of both their environment and external influences. This is not to say that the subject of a study can not be distinctive or even singular, far from it. Again, as with individuals, the response of any two communities to a given situation or development is never quite the same. The researcher must recognise that distinctiveness is the creation of many factors, not all of which originate within the group or area being studied. The only way to quantify, or even in many cases recognise, external influences is to look outside the area of study and compare it with others. The use of comparative data allows the local study to be fitted into the wider history of which it forms a part.

I

I am going to use as my first example an introduction to a study of the fictitious Ballymaturnip area of Belfast in the years before the First World War. This district lies south of the Lagan and at this time contained a large proportion of migrant labour, much of which was employed in the shipyards. A large part of the area was built on reclaimed land and the district as a whole consisted of streets of terraced parlour houses.

In these years the population of Ballymaturnip, in common with much of the rest of Belfast, lived in newly built terraced houses. However, general standards of health improved only slowly, if at all, and the death rate in the city remained high.

There appears to be a contradiction: the population was well housed but suffered poor health. General indicators of health, in the form of the city's death rate, (which is defined as the number dying per thousand inhabitants per year) and levels of child mortality (defined as the number of deaths within the first year of life per thousand live births), would seem to indicate that improvement was neither significant nor sustained in the later years of the nineteenth century.

Table 1: Infant Mortality and Death Rates in the city of Belfast, 1881-1905[1]

	Death rate	Infant Mortality
1881 – 1890	23.5	151
1891 – 1900	23.4	161
1901 – 1905	22.1	146

Certainly these figures do not present a very encouraging picture of conditions in Belfast during the years of the city's growth. However, for the statistics to be really meaningful we need to be able to compare Belfast with another area; that raises the problem of which city, or cities, to choose. The only urban centre in Ireland that compares with Belfast in terms of size is Dublin, but housing conditions and standards of health there were scandalously bad, even by contemporary standards. If all we want to do is prove that conditions in Belfast were comparatively good, then all we need do is compare the city's health record with that of Dublin.

But is this really a meaningful exercise? Belfast is an industrial city, thus it would be pertinent to discover how far it shared the problems associated with other industrialised centres of this period. A more reasonable comparison therefore would be with those centres in northern England and southern Scotland where economic and social conditions would be most similar (table two).

Although Belfast has the highest death rate in this sample, it is noticeable that its child mortality rate is almost the lowest. Once again there appears to be a contradiction. It could be suggested that the city's high levels of inward migration by adults in these years distorted the infant mortality rate. However, this was a feature of all industrial cities of this era and thus, while certainly a factor, migration cannot provide the full explanation.

Table 2: Infant Mortality and Death Rates in British Industrial Cities, 1896-1905[2]

	Death Rate	Infant Mortality
Barrow in Furness	14.9	144
Belfast	22.1	146 (b)
Birkenhead	18.4	167
Glasgow	20.4	149 (a)
Middlesbrough	21.6	182
Newcastle on Tyne	20.4	167
South Shields	19.1	156
Stockton on Tees	17.9	163
Sunderland	20.6	167

(a) 1891-1900 (b) 1901-1905

Child mortality is a good indicator of the general health conditions within a city, as it is influenced by a wide range of factors. The health and nutrition of the mother are critical elements in the survival of the child, as are factors such as housing, levels of health care and prevalence of disease. It might be useful to examine this aspect of Belfast's experience, using a slightly wider comparative group. This time I have included centres where migration might not be such an important factor and have also noted some international comparisons:

Table 3: Infant mortality in Belfast compared to British towns in 1904 and European Countries 1893-1902[3]

British Towns		European Countries	
Bristol	134	Ireland	104
London	144	Scotland	127
Belfast	154	Switzerland	145
Sheffield	158	The Netherlands	152
Dublin	168	England and Wales	152
Leeds	175	Belgium	157
Preston	185	France	158
Manchester	187	Italy	173
Liverpool	196	Spain	190
Birmingham	197	Germany	195

The results are quite surprising. Belfast has a far higher infant mortality rate than the Irish average, but this is to be expected when comparing an urban industrial population with a largely rural one in these years. However, although Belfast displays a higher rate than London, it compares well with other urban centres such as Manchester or Liverpool. The international comparisons present an even more complex picture, with Belfast coming only slightly below the average for Holland or England and Wales; in terms of infant mortality, Belfast appears surprisingly healthy compared to Spain or even Germany.

However, such comparisons can tell only half the story. We know now how Belfast compares with other centres, but what about variations in the health of the population within the city? Internal comparisons are perhaps even more important and revealing, explaining local variations within a study area. To make generalisations about a whole city, town, county or community is not only dangerously imprecise, but can often be misleading. There are social and economic divisions within any population, and their effects must be acknowledged and assessed. For example, did the average death rates discussed above disguise areas of higher mortality within the city? The answer might perhaps be found in the report of a 1914 committee examining conditions in the linen industry in Belfast. The report begins by breaking down the city's deaths by age group and then compares the death rates in different Dispensary Districts within the city.

Table 4: Death Rates (per 1000) of each age group in the city of Belfast[4]

	< 5 yrs	5-25	25-45	45-65	65 >
Belfast	45.67	4.45	9.8	28.33	73.8
Dispensary XII	49.7	4.63	11.37	25.2	72.53
Dispensary III	48.0	5.0	9.5	28.5	80.4
Dispensary V	57.0	5.69	15.9	39.0	80.73
Dispensary XV	72.0	5.14	10.93	49.1	56.9

Table 5: Belfast Health Data[5]

	Death Rate	Population Density	Birth Rate	Tuberculosis (Per 1000)
Belfast	17.2	26.3	28.4	2.07
Dispensary XII	17.2	36.0	35.5	2.44
Dispensary III	17.68	70.0	28.3	2.49
Dispensary V	23.15	112.0	31.9	2.66
Dispensary XV	23.38	106.0	28.9	3.17

As we can see, there are clearly defined local patterns in the death rates of these districts. The same variations also occur when looking at other indicators of general health in the city, suggesting that they are more than coincidental.

We need to explore what factors were affecting the basic health of those living in these areas of the city of Belfast in the early years of this century. The density of the population was clearly an influence, but the committee also suggests that the nature of employment was a significant factor in Belfast. Urban Dispensary XII, for example, which covered the area south of the Lagan and east of the Conniswater, was mainly inhabited by shipyard and engineering workers and contained few linen-workers. On the other hand, the area between the Crumlin and Shankill Roads, covered by dispensary III, contained a 'large number' of mill-workers. Districts V, between the Shankill and the Falls, and XV, between the Falls and the Grosvenor Roads, were respectively 'largely' and 'practically all' mill-workers.

The areas with the largest proportion of mill-workers saw high rates of child mortality (under five years) compared with the area where these workers were less prevalent. The population in these areas was far more densely crowded, reaching almost four times the average for the city as a whole in district V. Although the tuberculosis rates in all these working-class areas were higher than the average for the city as a whole, they are markedly higher in the mill districts. We can thus conclude that crowded living conditions and the widespread occurrence of industrial illness related to employment in the linen industry, increased the death rate in certain areas of the city. This in turn tended to push up the average figures for the city as a whole.

Was Belfast a healthy city? The answer clearly depends on how we interpret the word 'healthy', and on the basis of any comparisons. Compared to today, for example, Belfast at the start of the century was a very unhealthy place, but so too were all other cities. While Belfast had a high death rate compared to some other contemporary industrial centres, conditions appear less serious if the basis of the comparison is broadened. As noted earlier, within the city as a whole there was considerable variation in the standard of health between districts. This was caused not just by comparative inequalities in earnings but also by the community's employment pattern.

Once again such divisions are not unique to Belfast; if we look at another city with similar levels of housing and migration, we also find internal contrasts. At the turn of the century, and even today, Bristol is marked by sharp divisions in living and health standards. In outlying, mainly rural, areas such as Westbury or Stapleton or socially elite Clifton, conditions are far better than the poor and crowded St Philip or Central districts. This is due not just

Table 6: Health data for the city of Bristol[6]

	Population Density1913	Child Mortality 1911	Cases of TB 1913
Westbury	2.6	69	7
Stapleton	10.6	128	17
Knowle	19.8	103	26
Ashley	22.5	100	46
St George	29.9	152	68
Bedminster	31.8	143	89
Clifton	32.7	119	51
Central Ward	51.1	163	72
St Philip	82.7	164	96
BRISTOL	20.7	143	

to population density, but relates also to more general social and economic conditions in the locality.

How good was working class housing in Ballymaturnip, and Belfast in general, and how can we assess its quality? Perhaps a good starting point would be to ask what type of accommodation was typical of the city and how this compared with other centres. This should be assessed both in terms of the number of rooms a family rented and how many families were considered by the authorities to be living in overcrowded conditions.

Table 7: Percentage of total population occupying homes of each size 1905[7]

	1 Room	2 R	3 R	4 R	5 R +	Percentage Overcrowded
Belfast	0.4	4.7	6.4	29.1	59.4	8.29
Birmingham	0.3	2.4	29.4	13.0	54.9	10.33
Bristol	1.6	5.7	7.9	10.5	74.3	3.55
Dublin	24.7	21.0	10.3	10.1	33.9	31.71
Edinburgh	8.9	32.4	20.8	12.2	25.7	*
Glasgow	16.2	38.9	19.0	6.8	19.1	*
Leeds	0.4	9.5	16.0	25.0	49.1	10.08
Liverpool	2.7	5.9	8.8	18.4	64.2	7.94
London	6.7	15.2	16.6	15.2	46.0	16.01
Manchester	0.8	4.0	3.9	40.0	51.3	6.28
Preston	0.1	0.4	2.2	32.1	65.2	2.64
Sheffield	0.4	4.0	18.8	23.2	53.6	9.5

* The Scots did not calculate overcrowding in a comparable manner.

When compared to other urban centres, Belfast's housing in the early years of this century is very impressive, with almost 90 per cent of the population living in homes of four or more rooms compared to 25.9 per cent in Glasgow and 44 per cent in Dublin. However, although it appears that the housing was good, we also need to know whether it was expensive; did the Belfast resident have to pay higher rents than the Dubliner or Glaswegian for his home? The 'average' working-class home in Belfast was the four room kitchen or parlour house or the five-room parlour house. Such houses were built in tens of thousands during the final two decades of the nineteenth century, and are still common in the city. Rents varied considerably, depending on age and location, as the Board of Trade reported:

Four Room Kitchen House	3s to 4s a week
Four Room Parlour House	4s 6d to 5s a week
Five Room House	5s to 6s 3d a week [8]

Let us assume, arbitrarily, that a Belfast worker pays 5s for his new 'Parlour' house, what would residents of other cities have been able to obtain for the same price?

Birmingham } Manchester }	Largest of three room houses or smallest of the four-room houses.
Bristol	Similar to Belfast
Leeds } Preston }	A modern four room house or a back-to-back five-room house
Liverpool	Cheapest of the three- or four-room houses or tenements
Glasgow } London } Edinburgh }	Two rooms, in shared house or tenement block
Dublin	Three rooms, in shared house
Sheffield	Four-roomed house, not the best type. [9]

In these terms, the only city that can compare with Belfast is Bristol, where housing is also recognised as being unusually good. Compared to the appalling over-crowding of London, Glasgow or Dublin, we can say that the average Belfast family was very well housed. We must of course be careful not to apply inappropriate standards: 'very good' nineteenth-century working-class housing would seem very cramped to us today. Moreover, the definition of 'overcrowded' was more than two people to a room, thus a five-roomed house with ten people living in it was not deemed to be overcrowded.

Using such comparative data it is possible to see that late nineteenth-century Belfast was a healthier place than many other industrial cities, or indeed some European countries. Such comparisons do not take away from the distinctiveness of the city, but rather serve to explain and quantify it. They are also useful in drawing attention to questions that require further consideration. For example, why did the Belfast and Bristol industrial worker live in houses rather than tenement blocks like the Glaswegian? Why is child mortality in Belfast so far above the Irish average; was this just the effects of urban life or are there other factors? By addressing such questions, we are much better able to understand the experience of living in Belfast at the turn of the century.

Using these comparisons it is possible to re-write the introduction to the history of Ballymaturnip as follows:

> The standard of housing in Ballymaturnip, and in Belfast generally, was very high compared with similar industrial cities in Britain. Rents were lower, which meant that the industrial worker of the district was better housed than those of Glasgow, London or Leeds. Although Belfast's death rate was higher than that of many other industrial towns of this era, infant mortality was lower. In the case of Ballymaturnip, as with other areas where shipbuilding workers predominated, general standards of health were far better than those areas of the city where linen provided the main employment.

The inclusion of comparative data, both between areas of the city and with other centres, results in a much clearer understanding of the locality.

II

Comparative history can also lead to some very interesting and valuable conclusions in the study of a specific historical event. While working on another topic I became interested in enlistment in the armed forces during World War I from both Bristol and Belfast. I was investigating the frequently-heard claim that Belfast's losses had been disproportionately heavy. My first problem was to find a suitable sample comparison group, one which represented a cross section of contemporary society and yet was small enough to be manageable. I chose the employees of the councils in the two cities, who not only met this criteria, but whose experiences were also well documented.

In Bristol 1,527 council employees enlisted or were conscripted, of whom 167 were killed or died while in service (10.9 per cent). In Belfast 1,045 joined the armed forces voluntarily as conscription was never applied there, of these 133 lost their lives (12 per cent). The larger Bristol enlistment is due in part to conscription, but more importantly to the fact that the Bristol figure includes policemen (265) and teachers (201), neither of which category were council employees in Belfast.[10] This sample which I used for analysis compares with a total British army enlistment of 4,970,902, of whom 401,069 lost their lives from 1 November 1914 to 30 September 1918 (8 per cent).[11]

I compared the enlistment patterns of the council workers in the two cities to that of the army as a whole: was there a simple structural reason for the higher Belfast casualty rate? The results show that while about three-quarters of recruits from both cities served in the infantry, or as gunners or engineers, the proportion joining each arm of service was quite distinctive:

Table 8: Comparative data on Army Enlistment[12]

	Army Total 1914-1918	Army Recruits Only Bristol (a)	Bristol (b)	Belfast
Infantry	56.4%	42.6%	46.2%	67.3%
Cavalry	0.4%	2.2%	2.0%	4.8%
Artillery	13.8%	20.4%	13.1%	3.5%
Engineers	6.7%	14.7%	17.1%	5.4%
RASC/RAOC	7.5%	4.7%	5.4%	9.5%
RAMC	3.7%	6.5%	6.3%	6.6%

Bristol (a) total employees
Bristol (b) Minus police and teachers

Although the differences appear trivial, this distribution pattern was to have tragic consequences. Casualties were not evenly spread through the various branches of the army; only one in every hundred killed was a cavalryman, one in every forty was an engineer, but more than four out of five were infantrymen.[13] In simple terms, the larger the proportion of infantrymen a city sent to the front, the higher its casualties were likely to be. Bristol probably sent more men, but Belfast lost more, simply because so many of the recruits served in the infantry.

How typical were the cities' council workers of the population as a whole? Once again I needed comparative groups but in this case they did not have to be the same for each city. In the case of Belfast I chose a sample of twenty-four Presbyterian congregations who between them supplied 3,163 recruits,

426 of whom were killed or died (13.5 per cent). My reason for choosing this grouping was simple: the data were readily available in the official Roll of Honour of the Presbyterian Church.[14] In the case of Bristol I chose two schools, the small Church of England elementary school in the parish of St Nicholas with St Leonard and the prestigious Coulston Grammar School. During the war 831 former pupils of these institutions enlisted in the armed forces, 113 of whom lost their lives (13.6 per cent).[15] The social differences between the two schools can be deduced by the fact that whereas 26 per cent of 'old Colstonians' served at commissioned rank, only 3.9 per cent of those from the elementary school did.

Table 9: Comparative Enlistments Bristol and Belfast (%)

| | Bristol | | Belfast | |
	Council	Schools	Council	Churches
Infantry	42.6	43.9	64.9	55.9
Artillery	19.2	12.2	3.3	4.2
Engineers	13.9	6.6	5.2	6.0
Cavalry	2.1	6.8	4.6	3.0
RASC/RAOC	4.4	6.2	9.2	7.4
RAMC	6.2	3.1	6.4	4.0
Tank Corps	0.4	0.4	–	0.6
MG Corps	1.7	1.2	–	1.0
Navy/Marines	5.7	9.2	3.3	6.9
Air Force etc	3.7	5.6	1.4	2.9
Misc.	2.4	4.0	1.5	1.4

Table 10: Proportion of Casualties by Branch of Service (%)

| | Bristol | | Belfast | |
	Council	Schools	Council	Churches
Infantry	56.0	64.4	82.0	77.7
Artillery	22.8	15.9	2.3	2.1
Engineers	5.4	5.3	0.7	2.3
Cavalry	3.6	3.0	1.5	1.6
RASC/RAOC	1.2	0.9	1.5	2.3
RAMC	1.2	–	1.5	0.5
MG Corps	1.2	1.8	–	1.1
Navy/Marines	7.2	5.3	5.3	2.5
Air Force	1.2	2.7	–	0.7

Belfast did lose a disproportionate number of men during World War I, at least compared to Bristol, simply because a larger proportion of its recruits joined infantry units. This was merely an extension of pre-war recruiting practice; the Belfast district had always been a centre for infantry recruitment, with 63.9 per cent of those enlisting between 1904 and 1913 joining that branch compared to 47.6 per cent in Bristol.[16] The comparative aspect thus makes it possible not only to show that Belfast suffered higher than average losses, but also to identify the reasons.

III

One of the most striking differences I found between the cities I studied between 1880 and 1925, was in the bodies entrusted with the preservation of law and order. The police forces differed not only in terms of equipment and training, but also in their actual roles and recruitment patterns. Who were these men? What had they been before joining the police? How different were they to the communities they policed?

Belfast was policed by the Royal Irish Constabulary (RIC), a body established under the Irish Constabulary Act of 1822.[17] The city had it own borough police until 1864, when serious sectarian riots showed their inadequacy:

> The city of Belfast, with its mayor, town council, magistracy and its 'local police' were miserably incompetent to deal with sectarian outrage when the spark set the northern flax on fire. Occasionally an extra force of the constabulary had been sent to Belfast, not so much to preserve as to restore the peace of the town; for the mischief had been too often done before they arrived.[18]

The RIC differed from the policemen in the other cities in two ways. Firstly, they were part of a national force which could be rapidly reinforced from other areas or could send officers elsewhere in Ireland at short notice. Secondly, the RIC was primarily an armed force; although normally patrolling with batons, all members were equipped with and trained to use firearms. Between 1880 and 1925 the RIC was progressively equipped with Snider, Martini-Henry, Martini-Metford and finally Lee-Enfield carbines or rifles.[19] The RIC were to be the prototype for organisations such as the Palestinian and South African Police Forces. They were organised and equipped as a colonial gendarmerie rather than as 'normal' British policemen.

Although the RIC was based in Dublin, the city itself was not policed by them. The Dublin Metropolitan Police (DMP) were established as a result of extensive police reforms in 1836.[20] The members of the Dublin force were taller than the RIC, the minimum height being two inches greater, and better paid.[21] The 1,200 members of the DMP policed an area of thirty-six square miles and, unlike the RIC, were an unarmed force. The two forces were very different, as contemporaries noted:

> The officers of the DMP, with the exception of the commissioners, had all risen from the ranks, and in training the force was less military than the RIC and its men, who, in their large, silver-faced helmets embodied law and order with massive dignity. When in 1917 it was suggested that the two police forces might be amalgamated, the Chief Commissioner of the DMP strongly opposed the suggestion, pointing out that Dublin had special problems and that the DMP was a city force while the RIC was largely rural and semi-military.[22]

However, despite considerable similarities, Dublin's policemen were also distinctive from those of Bristol. The DMP was a government department and there was no involvement on the part of local government in running the city's police force. The Bristol Constabulary came into existence on 25 June 1836 with an establishment of 232 officers and constables.[23] The force slowly expanded as the city grew in size, until by 1906 there were 549 members. In 1902 the Chief Constable reported to the City Council's Watch Committee that the level of policing in the borough compared favourably with other large towns.[24] Although largely funded by government grants, the city of Bristol was in control of its police force and in normal circumstances there was no question of external interference. One of the few occasions when this did happen in Bristol was the Home Secretary's direct intervention in March 1900 to prevent the formation of a corps of police riflemen.[25] Although an armoury of pistols, cutlasses and lead-weighted truncheons was maintained at the Bridewell, Bristol police, like the DMP, were primarily an unarmed civilian force.

Where were policemen recruited? Again there appear to have been considerable differences between the forces. The DMP drew most of its recruits from social groups outside metropolitan Dublin, as a government enquiry heard in 1882:

> Q. Will you please tell us from what classes of the community recruits are usually drawn?
>
> A. As a general rule they are farmers sons and labourers, of course there are exceptions, a good man presenting himself and well recommended and possessing all the physical requirements, will not be rejected, although not from this class.

Q. From what parts of the country do most of these recruits come?

A. Generally from the Home Counties, from Wicklow, Meath, Kildare, Westmeath; but then as a matter of fact every other county is represented in the force.[26]

Thus the typical Dublin policemen was of rural origins, mostly from the surrounding counties, rather than a native of the city. The RIC drew the bulk of its recruits from the same source as the DMP, the sons of farmers and labourers. If it was unlikely that a Dubliner would be found policing his home city, the regulations of the RIC prohibited a Belfast policeman serving in his:

I do not get the same recruits that I send to the Depot. There is a regulation in the force that the men shall not serve in their own counties.[27]

There was a strong prejudice on the part of the RIC in favour of rural recruits and against those from Belfast, as appears in the evidence of Cooper Hadfield in 1882.

A. I am not speaking at all as to recruiting in Belfast, because very few join from Belfast.

Q. To what do you attribute that?

A. They are all of the artisan class in Belfast, and fully employed, sometimes a shop-assistant may offer himself for enrolment in the force, but I think they are the worst class for service, even though they are better educated than farmers sons. They are used to amusement and good eating and very seldom take kindly to the police force.[28]

If a man wished to join the RIC he had to obtain a recommendation from the local county inspector whose name was entered alongside that of the recruit in the force's register.[29] The recruit was then sent to Dublin for training, at which stage the unsuitable were to a large degree weeded out.[30] If the recruit was then sent to Belfast he could expect to serve there until he reached the rank of sergeant, unless he married a local woman, in which case he was transferred at once.[31]

The city of Bristol tended to recruit its policemen from the city and the surrounding counties rather than more distant areas. Between 1899 and 1913, 25 per cent of recruits gave their place of birth as Bristol, with the neighbouring counties of Somerset and Gloucestershire accounting for 35 per cent and 10.5 per cent respectively.[32] Thus the Bristol policeman was the most likely to come from the city itself or its surrounding area. All recruits had to be literate, under forty years of age, at least five feet seven, active, of good character and able to pass a medical examination.[33] The absence of a central training depot meant that recruits were quickly assigned to stations and the unsuitable had to be weeded out at that stage, dismissals for drunkenness were common and there were sometimes far more serious problems:

Earnest Tolly, 26 October 1904
On account of his filthy habits in his lodgings rendering him unfit for the force, ordered to resign forthwith.

Joseph William Dyer, 13 March 1907
For improperly working his beat being found in the grounds of a house at Stoke Hill on the 6th March 1907 and so conducting himself as to bring discredit upon the force. Allowed to resign forthwith.

Samuel Williams, 8 November 1907
For disreputable conduct which was revealed in a case of bastardry preferred against him at the police court on the 4th November 1907. Severely reprimanded and finally warned.

12 February 1908
For obtaining £10 from a servant girl and for general discreditable conduct, dismissed.

Francis John Hyde, 21 June 1911
For writing grossly indecent letters to a single woman on the 3rd of June 1911 and other dates. Dismissed the force.[34]

The Bristol police drew their manpower from a much wider range of employment backgrounds than the Irish police forces. Between 1899 and 1913 two thirds of the force gave their previous occupations as military (32.7 per cent), labourers (22.8 per cent) or skilled/semi-skilled workers (12.9 per cent).[35] A notable feature of Bristol's police recruitment in these years, compared to Ireland, is the high proportion of ex-soldiers.

Regardless of how similar the cities of Bristol and Belfast were in other ways, their policemen had little in common. They shared, along with the Dublin Metropolitan Police, the same basic function: the maintenance of law and order in an urban environment. However, the heavily armed, rurally-recruited RIC bore little comparison to the police forces of either Bristol or Dublin. Comparative studies can thus highlight distinctive local features.

Table 11: Police Recruitment of Ex-Soldiers 1899-1913[36]

Area	Total Recruits	% Ex-Soldier
City of London	1,039	26.1
London Metropolitan	18,670	14.0
Boroughs of England & Wales	39,175	21.7
Scottish Forces	7,748	10.6
Dublin Metropolitan	969	2.4
Royal Irish Constabulary	8,213	2.5
Total	75,814	16.4
Bristol	505	28.3

IV

There are of course limitations in the use of comparative studies in local history; in the main these are of a fairly practical nature. While it is valid to compare health and housing data between Belfast and British or indeed European industrial cities, the city can not be compared with rural districts of Ireland in a meaningful manner. Size is also important: Banbridge may have had a similar proportion of its labour force engaged in the linen industry as Belfast, but can it really be compared to that city, or to Manchester or Preston simply because they were also textile centres? It could however, be legitimately compared to a similar-sized community in the Lancashire cotton districts or Yorkshire woollen areas.

There are of course problems with comparative research which at times appear almost insoluble, notably if you are confronted by data in a language or format you are not able to understand. For instance, I was interested in imports of foodstuffs into Bristol and Belfast. In the case of Bristol I was quickly able to discover how many tons of flour, bacon, butter or lard were imported in 1880.[37] When I looked for a similar figure for Belfast I found a problem: imports figures are not given by weight but in terms of the containers in which they were packed. Thus instead of having my import figures in weights, I had them by volume, and many of the containers used had no apparent weight equivalent. The measures used in these lists included:

Hogshead   =   Barrel(52.5 gallons)
Box   =   ?
Tierces   =   Barrel(42 gallons)
Barrels   =   (31.5 gallons)
Firkin   =   Barrel (8 gallons)
Keg   =   Barrel (?)[38]

Clearly, unless I could find a definition for kegs and boxes, and above all a figure for what a gallon would weigh, it would not be possible to convert the data into usable form. The nearest standard I could find was that a barrel of herrings contained either 212 or 235 lbs, depending on how it was packed, and a tierce 304 to 336 lbs. When these weights are divided by the capacity of the barrels the gallon may have weighed 6.7lb, 7.5lb, 7.2lb or 8lb. I decided to adopt an average of 7.5lb to the gallon cubic capacity. As for the box, I found that it was defined, in terms of herrings, as a quarter of a barrel, so I allowed 58lbs. The keg? I knew one of gunpowder weighed 100lb so I accepted this as a rough figure:

Hogshead	=	452.5 lbs		Box	=	58 lbs
Tierce	=	315 lbs		Keg	=	100 lbs
Barrel	=	236 lbs		Firkin	=	60 lbs

Such rule of thumb calculation cannot be precise, as gallons (8 pints) of flour, bacon or lard will weight different amounts. This is due simply to the density of the material involved and a great deal of practical experiment would be necessary to find a real figure. However, these standard weights did allow me to calculate approximate figures for food imports in these years. If such a problem was still further complicated by the document being written in a shorthand form (Hhds, Tc, Bl [also used for bale], Frk, Bx), or old-fashioned script, then the task of the researcher is still more difficult. Will a Russian barrel hold the same as an Irish one? Irish measures are not exactly the same as English ones; a French keg of gunpowder contains twice as much as an English one. Such differences must always be considered, and they represent a great danger for the unwary researcher.

It is important not be too ambitious. Certain comparisons may be attractive and relevant but not really practical in view of the researcher's personal knowledge and abilities. You could, for example, legitimately compare the fishing industry of Donegal with that of the Basque region of Spain. The two areas appear enticingly similar, but is your Spanish good enough to use official reports, or your Basque language good enough to understand local literature and folklore on the subject? Official statistics, which are similar in all languages, may allow you to compare the number of boats, average size, number of crew and size of catch, but they do not give any real view of the social structures. If you have a good working knowledge of Spanish and Basque the comparison is a good one; if not why not consider Cornwall or the west coast of Scotland?

A comparison of local government in Belfast and Dublin may appear an attractive project, but how feasible is it? It is not just a question of availability of comparative data, but the sheer scale of such an undertaking. How many volumes would it require to cover this topic from 1700 to the present day? The only way to make this practical would be to set a time limit – add 1890-1914 to the title. Alternatively, reduce the scope of the study: 'Local Government attitudes to Unemployment in Belfast and Dublin'. Always pick a subject that you can undertake in the time available, not perhaps what you really want to do, but rather what you know you can do.

Do not approach a comparison with the single thought of proving how different the two places were – this will only tend to distort your results. You do not have to prove that Belfast is unique by showing how different it is to Moscow; the interesting thing is the degree of similarity. No city is totally distinctive from every other, but equally, every urban conurbation is singular. The great advantage of comparative data is that it allows the researcher to identify and to a degree quantify those aspects which give a centre or community its singularity. For this reason the local historian should never be afraid to look beyond the immediate area of interest.

1. *Belfast Health Commission: Report to the Local Government Board of Ireland* [Cd 4128] H. C. 1908 xxxi pp. 13, 21.
2. *Report of an enquiry by the Board of Trade into working class rents, housing and retail prices* [Cd 3864] H.C. 1908 cvii.
3. Anon, *Infant Mortality: An inquiry into its causes and how it might be reduced, with special reference to the city of Belfast* (Belfast, 1906), pp. 5-6.
4. *Report of the Departmental Committee on humidity and ventilation in flax mills and linen factories* [Cd 7433 & 7446] H.C. 1914 xxxvi tables C-E.
5. *Report of the Departmental Committee on humidity and ventilation in flax mills and linen factories* [Cd 7433 & 7446] H.C. 1914 xxxvi tables C-E.
6. *Report of Bristol City Council Medical Officer of Health* (1911); *Bristol Adult School, Facts about Bristol's Social life* (Bristol, 1914), pp.1-2.
7. *Working Class Rents and Housing* H.C. 1908 cvii, Appendix II.
8. *Working Class Rents and Housing* H.C. 1908 cvii, Appendix II.
9. *Working Class Rents and Housing* H.C. 1908 cvii, Appendix I.
10. Bristol: Roll of Honour, Bristol Record Office, Access No 40342; Belfast: Commemorative plaques in Belfast City Hall; In Council Chamber – Roll of Honour; Ground Floor Hall –North Irish Horse; First Floor Hall – Those who died, Roll of Gas Workers.
11. *General Annual Reports of the British Army* [Cd 1193] H.C. 1921.
12. *General Annual Reports of the British Army* [Cd 1193] H.C. 1921.
13. *General Annual Reports of the British Army* [Cd 1193] H.C. 1921.
Percentage of total killed/died 1914-18

Infantry	82.8
Artillery	7.3
Engineers	2.5
RASC/RAOC	1.6
Cavalry	1.0
RAMC	0.9
Labour Corps	0.8.

14. Roll of Honour of the Irish Presbyterian Church.
15. The Rolls of Honour of both schools can be found in the Bristol Central Library.
16. *Annual Reports of Army Recruiting* (1904-1913).
17. J. K. Sinclair, & F. Scully, *Arresting memories* (Belfast, 1982), Introduction.
18. R. Curtis, *History of the Royal Irish Constabulary* (Dublin, 1869), chapter XVI.
19. Charles Townshend, *The British campaign in Ireland* (Oxford, 1978) pp. 42-3; Charles Townshend, *Political violence in Ireland* (Oxford, 1983) pp. 74-7.
20. R. B. McDowell, *The Irish Administration* (London 1964), p. 138.
21. *Commission on Royal Irish Constabulary and Dublin Metropolitan Police* [Cd 7421] H.C. 1914, xliv.
22. McDowell, *Administration*, pp. 144-5.

23. R. Walters, *Establishment of the Bristol Police Force* (Bristol, 1975), p. 1.
24. Bristol Record Office, Chief Constables Report Books, Vol 1, 29 Oct 1902 Acc No 34908(2) a+b:

Town		Per Police Constable	
	Population	Acres of Town	Miles of Road
Nottingham	826	37.75	$\frac{5}{8}$
Hull	679	25.5	$\frac{1}{3}$
Manchester	540	12.75	$1\frac{1}{2}$
Leeds	857	43	$\frac{3}{4}$
Southampton	788	39	$1\frac{1}{5}$
Cardiff	668	25	$\frac{1}{2}$
Birmingham	653	18	$\frac{1}{3}$
Liverpool	509	11.25	$\frac{1}{3}$
Plymouth	800	18.5	$\frac{1}{2}$
Sheffield	799	46	$\frac{3}{4}$
Bradford	716	58.33	1
Newcastle	671	16.75	$\frac{5}{8}$
Bristol	639	22	$\frac{1}{2}$

25. B. Howells, *Police in late Victorian Bristol* (Bristol, 1989), p. 10.
26. *Dublin Metropolitan Police-Report of the Committee of Enquiry* [Cd 3577] H.C. 1883 xxxii, Questions 151 & 156.
27. *Belfast Riot Commission*, [Cd 4925] H.C. xviii Question 694.
28. *Royal Irish Constabulary-Report of the Committee of Enquiry* [Cd 3576] H.C. 1883 xxxii, Questions 286-7.
29. Townshend, *Campaign in Ireland*, p. 45.
30. *Commission on Royal Irish Constabulary and Dublin Police.*
31. *Belfast Riot Commission*, question 701-3.
32. Bristol Record Office, Constable Books of Bristol Police Force, Acc. No 34908(6) a+b:

Area	Recruits	% Total
Bristol	127	25.0
Somerset	178	35.1
Gloucestershire	54	10.6
South-Western counties	55	10.8
Other English counties	50	9.9
Wales	28	5.5
Ireland	12	2.4
Overseas	3	0.6

33. Howell, *Police in late Victorian Britain,* p. 9.
34. Bristol Record Office, Constable Books, pp. 590, 635, 692, 694.
35. Bristol Record Office, Constable Books:

Soldier, Royal Navy, Royal Marine	32.7%
Labourer	22.8%
Skilled/Semi-Skilled Worker	12.9%
Railway Worker	5.9%
Police, Fireman, Postman, Tram Worker	5.0%
Domestic/Hotel Servant	4.8%
Miner/Quarryman	4.5%
Clerks	3.6%
Warehouse/Transport	3.4%
Merchant Navy	1.8%
Shopworkers	1.4%
Misc (inc Farmers)	1.2%

36. *Annual Reports of the Director General of Army Recruiting*; Bristol Record Office, Constable Books of Bristol Police Force.
37. *Bristol Docks Committee Annual Report* (1913).
38. *Annual Report of the Belfast Harbour Commissioners* (1880).